White Educators Negotiating Complicity

Philosophy of Race

Series Editor: George Yancy, Emory University

Editorial Board: Sybol Anderson, Barbara Applebaum, Alison Bailey, Chike Jeffers, Janine Jones, David Kim, Emily S. Lee, Zeus Leonardo, Falguni A. Sheth, Grant Silva

The Philosophy of Race book series publishes interdisciplinary projects that center upon the concept of race, a concept that continues to have very profound contemporary implications. Philosophers and other scholars, more generally, are strongly encouraged to submit book projects that seriously address race and the process of racialization as a deeply embodied, existential, political, social, and historical phenomenon. The series is open to examine monographs, edited collections, and revised dissertations that critically engage the concept of race from multiple perspectives: sociopolitical, feminist, existential, phenomenological, theological, and historical.

Recent Titles in the Series

White Educators Negotiating Complicity: Roadblocks Paved with Good Intentions, by Barbara Applebaum
White Ignorance and Complicit Responsibility: Transforming Collective Harm Beyond the Punishment Paradigm, by Eva Boodman
Iranian Identity, American Experience: Philosophical Reflections on Race, Rights, Capabilities, and Oppression, by Roksana Alavi
The Weight of Whiteness: A Feminist Engagement with Privilege, Race, and Ignorance, by Alison Bailey
The Logic of Racial Practice: Explorations in the Habituation of Racism, edited by Brock Bahler
Hip-Hop as Philosophical Text and Testimony: Can I Get a Witness?, by Lissa Skitolsky
The Blackness of Black: Key Concepts in Critical Discourse, by William David Hart
Self-Definition: A Philosophical Inquiry from the Global South and Global North, by Teodros Kiros
A Phenomenological Hermeneutic of Antiblack Racism in The Autobiography of Malcolm X, by David Polizzi
Buddhism and Whiteness, edited by George Yancy and Emily McRae
Black Christology and the Quest for Authenticity: A Philosophical Appraisal, by John H. McClendon III
For Equals Only: Race, Equality, and the Equal Protection Clause, by Tina Fernandes Botts
Politics and Affect in Black Women's Fiction, by Kathy Glass
The Habits of Racism: A Phenomenology of Racism and Racialized Embodiment, by Helen Ngo

White Educators Negotiating Complicity

Roadblocks Paved with Good Intentions

Barbara Applebaum

LEXINGTON BOOKS
Lanham • Boulder • New York • London

Published by Lexington Books
An imprint of The Rowman & Littlefield Publishing Group, Inc.
4501 Forbes Boulevard, Suite 200, Lanham, Maryland 20706
www.rowman.com

86-90 Paul Street, London EC2A 4NE

Copyright © 2022 by The Rowman & Littlefield Publishing Group, Inc.

All rights reserved. No part of this book may be reproduced in any form or by any electronic or mechanical means, including information storage and retrieval systems, without written permission from the publisher, except by a reviewer who may quote passages in a review.

British Library Cataloguing in Publication Information Available

Library of Congress Cataloging-in-Publication Data Available

ISBN: 978-1-66690-415-4 (cloth : alk. paper)
ISBN: 978-1-66690-417-8 (pbk. : alk. paper)
ISBN: 978-1-66690-416-1 (electronic)

Contents

Acknowledgments	vii
1 White Complicity	1
2 The Entangled Armor of White Complicity: Innocence and Ignorance	23
3 Toward a Vigilantly Vulnerable Informed Humility	55
4 When White Educators Are Part of the Problem	89
5 Cultivating a Vigilantly Vulnerable Informed Humility	121
Bibliography	131
Index	143
About the Author	147

Acknowledgments

That we are epistemically interdependent has long become a tenet of feminist philosophizing. As communities of knowers, we engage with others' ideas, we inspire each other, and build on others' work. Such interdependence mirrors the intersubjectivity of our lives, those relationships that make life worth living. This is good. I have always found the Hebrew word *Hakarat HaTov* fundamental to life because it means both recognizing the good and an appreciation of the good that one has been gifted. *Hakarat HaTov* ensures that support and assistance are not taken for granted. It makes sense, then, that acknowledgments come at the beginning of a book to express awareness and an appreciation of the role that others have played in bringing such a project to fruition.

First and foremost, I express my *Hakarat HaTov* to George Yancy whose own work reverberates in the pages of this book. His writings not only inspired and continue to inspire my own, but his encouragement and support have made positive contributions to my academic journey, my pedagogy, and how I understand my role in the social world. I believe we all owe him a debt of gratitude for all he risks in his attempts to make the world a more just place.

In addition, my thanks go out to the many scholars upon whose shoulders this book stands. While they are too many to name individually, a few deserve noteworthy mention. Thank you to Alison Bailey whose beautifully crafted arguments have always allowed me to understand more clearly something yet hidden to me. A deep gratitude to Kristie Dotson, Gaile Pohlhaus Jr., and Nora Berenstain who continue to take me on intellectual journeys around the complexities of epistemic injustice. Although I have never personally met them, I feel like I know them through their works. Any student who studies with me has become familiar with your names and the conceptual clarity you bring to the topics you write about.

Thank you to my colleagues and students in Cultural Foundations of Education who not only offer me a supporting environment in which I can flourish but also critique me with care. Special thanks to Maryann Barker, our office manager, without whom the administrative parts of my job would be so much more onerous that they would impinge on the time I have available for my academic efforts.

Deep gratitude to Jana Hodges-Kluck and Sydney Wedbush for their excellent guidance through the publishing process.

Some sections of chapters 4 and 5 are expanded portions of articles previously published: Reprinted by permission from Springer Nature: Spring Nature, *Studies in Philosophy and Education*, "Ongoing Challenges for White Educators Teaching White Students about Whiteness." *Studies in Philosophy and Education* 40, no. 4 (2021): 429–441, https://doi.org/10.1007/s11217-021-09771-y, Copyright © 2021 and Barbara Applebaum, "The Non-Performativity of White Virtue-Signaling: Insights for Social Justice Pedagogy," *Philosophy of Education 77*, no. 3 (2021).

To my special friends whose support I am blessed with, thank you for the emotional cocoon you make possible and that helps me get through challenging times.

Finally, I want to express my deepest affection to my family, those here and those no longer with me, because family, with all its ups and downs, is one of the most important and precious gifts in my life.

Chapter 1

White Complicity

In his powerful op-ed piece in the *New York Times* entitled "Dear White America," George Yancy[1] challenges white people to consider how they are implicated in systemic white supremacy. In this letter, Yancy invites white people to honestly engage with their deepest assumptions, emotional habits, and patterns of practices and to consider how they are complicit with white systemic and institutional power and privilege. As he explains,

> You are part of a system that allows you to walk into stores where you are not followed, where you get to go for a bank loan and your skin does not count against you, where you don't need to engage in 'the talk' that black people and people of color must tell their children when they are confronted by white police officers.[2]

Even whites who are well-intentioned, Yancy argues, benefit from racism and, thus, are implicated in ways they may not yet understand. Yancy offers that as a man, he is sexist because he benefits from sexism even if that is not his intention. Similarly, white people are complicit in racism, even when they might have good intentions. Most significantly, Yancy points to the relationality of whiteness: "As you reap comfort from being white, we suffer for being black and people of color . . . your comfort is linked to our pain and suffering."[3]

Regardless that the letter was written in a tone of love, the vitriolic backlash Yancy received because of the letter became the context for his next book, *Backlash: What Happens When We Talk Honestly about Racism in America*.[4] As he chronicles the writing of the letter and the menacing, personal trauma resulting from its aftermath, and as he processes what this means, Yancy repeatedly elucidates that his intention was to introduce different ways of seeing the world and encouraging white people to see themselves differently in relationship to that world, especially the ways in which they are embedded within a white supremacist world which they perpetuate and benefit from.[5]

The concept of white[6] complicity is mentioned or implied in the long history of Black intellectuals who theorize on the nature of whiteness and the ways it is manifested in everyday life.[7] The concept is also prominent in the scholarship of feminists of color who critique feminism for its whiteness.[8] Recently, the topic of white complicity has been addressed in discussions of whiteness in post-apartheid South Africa.[9]

To begin to address the concept of white complicity, two points must be briefly enunciated. First, the concept of race that is implied is not primarily about biology but rather understood as a socially constructed category in which racial groups are mutually constituted through normalization processes where one group becomes the measure against which all other groups are evaluated as "different" or "deficient." While race is a socially constructed concept, it has very real material effects. In terms of whiteness, although the definition is difficult to pin down,[10] Ruth Frankenberg offers that whiteness is

> a location of structural advantage, of race privilege. Second it is a "standpoint," a place from which White people look at ourselves, at others, and at society. Third, "Whiteness" refers to a set of cultural practices that are usually unmarked and unnamed.[11]

Cheryl Harris[12] suggests that whiteness is best understood as a form of property rights that is systemically protected by social institutions such as law. The reference to property rights highlights that white people have an *investment* in whiteness that can obscure how white people, even with good intentions, are complicit in sustaining a racially unjust system.

For the purposes of this project, I define whiteness as a system or social structure that is built around a racial ideology that operates to justify relations of racial dominance and subordination. Thus, whiteness is understood to not just be about the color of one's skin but intimately related to the *construction of race* within systems of power and privilege. Moreover, the meaning of whiteness is constituted through the process of negation of what is outside its borders. Jonathan Warren and France Winddance Twine explain this reality as the "binary oppositional logic of racial politics in the United States" in which Black Americans "represent the racialized other against which Whiteness takes shape."[13] Whiteness means nothing without the existence of what is non-white, the center and periphery are mutually constituted. As

Yancy intimates in the first paragraph of this chapter, whiteness is inherently relational.

Second, and related to the above, the understanding of racism grounding white complicity is not exclusively about individuals' prejudiced attitudes. Rather, white complicity stems from an awareness of the institutional and cultural practices that generate and maintain a racially unjust system from which individual prejudice and implicit bias arise. This point is effectively captured by Yancy when he underscores that racism is not solely "a site of individual acts of meanness," but rather is more about "a complex web of racist power relationships . . . (and) heteronomous webs of white practices" to which white people "are linked both as a beneficiary and as co-contributor to such practices."[14] I use the term "systemic white supremacy" because it more clearly reveals the interrelated dynamics between social structures, individuals, and power that are required for being able to recognize white complicity.

Systemic white supremacy is not exclusively about the self-conscious racism of white supremacist hate groups but, more precisely, as Charles Mills[15] explains, white supremacy is the unnamed *system* against which those who are non-white are measured. Frances Lee Ansely's definition of systemic white supremacy, often cited to define the term as it is used by critical race scholars, emphasizes this point. By white supremacy, Ansely refers to

> a political, economic and cultural system in which whites overwhelmingly control power and material resources, conscious and unconscious ideas of white superiority and entitlement are widespread, and relations of white dominance and non-white subordination are daily reenacted across a broad array of institutions and social settings.[16]

Similarly, David Gillborn defines white supremacy as "a comprehensive condition whereby the interests and perceptions of white subjects are continually placed centre stage and assumed as 'normal.'"[17]

The advantage of employing the term "systemic white supremacy" is that the systematicity of racism that privileges whites is brought to the forefront. Racism is not exclusively about individual bad attitudes or inaccurate beliefs but about how these attitudes, beliefs, and practices are connected to a realm of social and structural power. Another way of putting this follows the metaphor of shifting the focus from "some bad apples" to the "bad barrel" and how the barrel is managed and maintained. To solely locate racism with those who are explicitly racist, "the bad apples," allows the system of racial oppression, "the barrel," to be obscured and, thus, shields the system from challenge. More significantly, well-intentioned people can avoid having to consider their complicity in systemic racial injustice because being racist is assumed to be about someone else. After the inhumane murder of George Floyd at the hands of former police officer Derek Chauvin who knelt on Floyd's neck for over 9 minutes while Floyd is screaming, "I can't breath," many white people were finally willing to criticize individual instances of police brutality against Black bodies. However, few white people were ready to acknowledge and dismantle the structural features of unjust institutions, such as the police that create the context where police brutality is "rationalized" as necessary and where police brutality is protected from accountability. While there was a growing willingness to condemn individual police officers as bad apples, there is much less willingness to critique the police as an institution, a bad barrel, that supports bad apples.

Mills explains that white supremacy, like the concept of patriarchy, makes power relations visible and ties together what might seem like isolated practices and events to patterns produced by an unjust system. Finally, systemic white supremacy underscores that racism is not an anomaly within a polity that is basically egalitarian but an everyday phenomenon that is part of the seemingly normal workings of a social system. When racism is understood as exclusively about having a set of prejudiced beliefs, stereotypes, or negative attitudes toward marginalized racial groups, this narrow and individualist focus conceals the deep ways that one can be complicit and is especially problematic because it diverts attention from the ways in which "good white people" are implicated in maintaining a system of racial injustice.

This definition of systemic white supremacy makes it feasible to understand how racial injustice could be reproduced by well-intentioned white individuals, people who might believe that they are paragons of antiracism. Consequently, for white individuals, "being good" must be critically and vigilantly scrutinized because believing that one is good/innocent often serves to immunize one from considering one's complicity in systems of racial injustice and, furthermore, contributes to shielding the unjust system from challenges. This echoes Audrey Thompson's assertion that white ethical sensibilities can serve as "one of the main obstacles to racial change."[18]

My research, as a white educator, has focused on white complicity in the context of higher education and, more precisely, how well-intentioned white students engage patterns of discursive practices of denial and avoidance to insulate themselves from having to examine their individual and collective roles in the perpetuation of systemic racial oppression and privilege. The tenacity of white denials of complicity encompasses white denials of racism, on the one hand, but also defenses of white innocence, on the other. Research has shown that white denials of complicity are experienced as violence by many students of color, as will be further addressed in subsequent chapters. Moreover, such defensive, discursive moves on the part of white students thwart the possibility of engaged cross-racial dialogue in the classroom. My previous research attempts to understand what fuels the persistent and commonplace resistance of white students to seriously engage with what students of color are saying about their experiences with racism in the world, on campus, and in our own classroom.

While white students and their complicity in systemic white supremacy has been extensively explored, in this book I turn the attention to the complicity of white educators in higher education who teach about and interrogate whiteness with a racially diverse group of students. This becomes especially complicated given that white educators who acknowledge complicity are not situated outside of the problem of whiteness and are agents of the same insidious practices that studies on white complicity demarcate. In her profoundly insightful article "Tiffany, Friend of People of Color: White Investments in Antiracism," Audrey Thompson addresses the problematic nature of keeping whiteness at the center of antiracism and antiracist education. Thompson thoughtfully and critically reflects on how "progressive white professors . . . (who) pride themselves on 'getting' race issues"[19] are subject to the dangers of thinking themselves to be exceptional whites in the ways they write and talk authoritatively about whiteness. She maintains that "progressive whites must interrogate the very ways of being good . . . for the moral framing that gives whites credit for being antiracist is parasitic on the racism that it is meant to challenge."[20]

Building on Thompson's arguments, in this book I continue the scrutiny of white educators who teach about and interrogate whiteness emphasizing the complicated effects of white complicity on pedagogy. What does it mean to be a white educator teaching about whiteness to a racially diverse group of students while simultaneously acknowledging one's white complicity? How does complicity create challenges for pedagogy? How do white educators continue to both benefit from and contribute to the perpetuation and management of whiteness through our/their[21] pedagogy while at the same time aiming to be vigilant about our/their complicity?

Even writing about white educators is a recentering of whiteness. In her discussion of epistemic oppression, Kristie Dotson cautions, "When addressing and identifying forms of epistemic oppression one needs to endeavor not to perpetuate epistemic oppression."[22] This is complicated because as Fiona Probyn-Rapsey[23] contends that whites studying whiteness while trying not to reinscribe whiteness is a paradox. Dotson's and Probyn-Rapsey's comments serve an unambiguous reminder of the ways in which even in our scholarly endeavors to disrupt systemic white supremacy, we can reproduce it. The question that motivates this book is what can it mean to teach against whiteness when one lives the paradox that Probyn-Rapsey describes? What can it mean to be a white educator teaching about whiteness while constituted by the very thing one is trying to critique?

The arguments in this book aim less at providing definitive answers. My objective, instead, is to raise questions that seek to initiate discussion about conflicts regarding white pedagogical values that are often not critically addressed: What are the pedagogical dilemmas that arise when white educators teach and interrogate whiteness with a racially diverse group of students? How might the pedagogy of white educators, despite aiming to disrupt whiteness, continue to further normalize and reproduce its hegemonic power in the classroom? At the end of my last book, I pondered, "Do I implement what I argue for theoretically?"[24] This book attempts to address this question, in a sense, and thus, what I write, although theoretical, has deep personal implications for me and my pedagogy.

There is a growing body of research around the complicity of white educators, especially in teacher education. In what follows, I note one study that explicitly deals with white educator complicity because it highlights the costs for students of color of such complicity. In "Complicity, Responsibility, and Authorization: A Praxis of Critical Questioning for White Literacy Educators," Julia Daniels and Heather Hebart[25] explore their own complicity and responsibility during moments of racialized violence occurring in their classrooms, those recurring instances of white students expressing ideas or feelings that delegitimize the experiences of their students of color. They recognize the implication of the white educator in the construction of such moments and "in the creation of a classroom environment that gives (implicit or explicit) permission or 'authorization' . . . for such moment to emerge and reverberate."[26]

Daniels and Hebart reflect not only on the ways they can help their white students more critically engage with their whiteness, but they are also focused on the ways in which white educators can support students of color in those moments. Offering a praxis of reflexive questioning as a heuristic for possible responses to such racialized violence in the classroom, Daniels and Hebart's research is notable for both considering white complicity as well as the violence it produces on students of color. Some of the reflexive questions they recommend are the following:

> How have I framed what counts as knowledge and knowledge creation in this classroom?
> How have I authorized particular patterns of communication and ways of communicating?
> How have I framed the differential risks and responsibilities of learning and participation?
> What am I communicating to my students about language and how language works in this classroom?[27]

My work builds on this growing body of research by reflecting upon some of the complicated conflicts that white educators encounter in doing social justice education.

Although not directly concerned with the area of pedagogy, Zak Foste[28] models a white researcher whose acknowledged complicity leads him to advance new types of reflexivity for white researchers studying whiteness. He asks, "What does it mean to be a white person researching whiteness?"[29] Using his own qualitative research project, Foste demonstrates how white researchers remain complicit in the reproduction of whiteness even when their aim is to disrupt its hegemonic force. He suggests that white researchers reflect on how they create contexts of racial comfort with their informants, how they unintentionally validate racist beliefs, and to deeply consider when opportunities for educational interventions are avoided. Similarly, the target of this book project is white academics who in negotiating their complicity reflexively question what means to be a white educator teaching about whiteness to a racially diverse group of students while negotiating their complicity.

In the remainder of this chapter, I will address the meaning of white complicity and clarify why traditional approaches that address the concept of complicity cannot capture the unique features of white complicity. One of the claims of white complicity is that all whites are complicit, a claim that has provoked much controversy. I will argue that opposing the idea that all white people are complicit presumes transcendence from the racist system. Briefly reviewing some of the research on the different discursive ways that white complicity is denied, and the consequences and effects of such denials, will help me to dispute the "not all whites are racist" rejoinder. I maintain that the premise that all whites are complicit can help minimize those (even if it cannot eliminate all) consequences and effects that result from white denials of complicity. Subsequently, acknowledging white complicity provides white people with a different framework to understand whiteness. In other words, acknowledging complicity offers a lens for better attending to what people of color say about the oppressive experiences they endure. Finally, a summary of the book chapters will be described.

WHAT IS WHITE COMPLICITY?

Scholars in philosophy and in legal studies have long focused on complicity or accomplice liability with the aim of explaining how a person can be accountable and responsible for the wrongful conduct of another. Significant and thoughtful expansions upon this scholarship have been able to encompass more circumstances of complicity. Among the many excellent accounts, I mention Christopher Kutz's[30] discussion of participatory intentions that aims to elucidate the meaning and ethics of complicity in collective wrongdoing. As I write, the complicity of elected officials in the United States, supporters of former president Donald Trump, conservative media outlets, and law enforcement in the insurrection that occurred on the Capitol Building in Washington D.C. on January 6, 2021, is being debated. I am certain these philosophical developments around the meaning of complicity and responsibility can be helpful in these deliberations, at least at the scholarly level.

Even extended conceptions of complicity and responsibility, however, are ineffective for apprehending white complicity. White complicity brings to the forefront the ways in which white people through their constitution as white, through discursive practices of denial that are systemically authorized, and by benefiting from white privilege contribute to the maintenance of systemic racial injustice. From this perspective, all white people, regardless of one's good intentions and whether they are consciously aware of the effects of their practices or not, must continually consider the ways in which they are implicated in the perpetuation of systemic white supremacy.

The topic of white complicity arises in a context that is distinct from the type of cases of complicity that serve as the point of reference for conventional analyses of complicity. I highlight four aspects of divergence that clarify the distinctiveness of white complicity from other forms of complicity. First, the immediate contrast involves the *clear consensus of wrongdoing* in many of the central cases taken up by scholars studying complicity that is absent when addressing white complicity. While the "what"[31] of complicity seems clear in many studies of complicity, there is still widespread reluctance to acknowledge the wrongness of systemic white supremacy. Put differently, discussions around complicity often focus on the *connection* between an individual's or group of individuals' action or inaction and the wrongdoing of others. The wrongdoing itself, however, remains undisputed. In the context of white complicity, it is the connection between the agent and the system that colludes in keeping injustice concealed to those who benefit or who can remain comfortable because of this concealment. Thus, exposing the connection or relationship between the agent and the system/structures of injustice, which is what the concept of white complicity is meant to unmask, also serves to expose systemic wrongdoing and the way it is maintained. When Mark Sanders[32] argues that addressing complicity can provide a basis for progressive resistance, it is because acknowledging white complicity is a form of social critique that exposes how injustice is normalized.

A second distinctive feature of white complicity involves the conception of the agent and the practices presumed. White complicity highlights discursive practices that are not an aberration or exception from "normal" behavior but encompasses the quotidian,[33] everyday practices of white people that do not necessarily appear to be problematic to the perpetrator. In the scholarship with which I engage in this book, white people are *direct* agents of harm even though the harm arises through being embedded within an unjust system and might not even be visible to the perpetrator. In exposing the normalizing of injustice through everyday practices, white complicity presumes an interrelationship between individuals and the social structures that constitute them. Moreover, white complicity cannot be attended to without addressing power dynamics. Structures of power and knowledge constitute us as actors and our collective practices, in turn, can support or disrupt those social structures. Thus, white complicity is not a form of complicity in *another's* wrongdoing but comprises complicity of *one's own actions or inactions* in structures that constitute one and that simultaneously maintain injustice.

Afxentis Afxentiou, Robin Dunford, and Michael Neu[34] helpfully articulate how conventional approaches to complicity presume an atomistic individual, a subject that is an abstract unit, not contingent on any historical, social, or political features. Presuming an abstract individual entails ignoring how we are constituted in relation. This social ontology disregards how being white has harmful implications for what it means not to be white. Such an individualistic approach to complicity fails to capture white complicity that presumes subjects who are situated and embedded in social, historical, and political contexts. Atomistic complicity covers up the reality of white complicity because whiteness itself can be ignored and, thus, remain unchallenged.

When the positionality of the subject does not arise for consideration in definitions of complicity, a strong emphasis on the *accomplice's intentions* often serves as the primary criteria for participation in wrongdoing. Consequently, accomplice complicity also depends on *what the accomplice knows* or *can be reasonably expected to know* about the wrongdoing. To be complicit, then, is to act intentionally in some way, or, minimally, recklessly, or negligently (because one should have known). It follows that the accomplice could avoid complicity and is, therefore, liable, or blameworthy. As will be extensively elucidated in later chapters, white complicity is more about discursive effects than intentions and white complicity is camouflaged by white ignorance where ignorance seemingly appears to white people as knowledge. This entails that white complicity cannot be avoided so long as the system of whiteness remains intact.

In his discussion of public inquiries and methods, Owen Thomas explains how individualistic approaches to complicity can articulate the connection between "bad apples" and past wrongs. However, what such approaches neglect is "an account of the 'bad barrel'—structures of power and knowledge that constitute us as actors inclined to behave in a particular way in the first place."[35] For Thomas, focusing on who is individually to blame diverts attention from unjust systems which can remain shielded from contestation. When assigning blame is the aim of definitions of complicity, structures of power that affect and are affected by what individuals do or fail to do are ignored. Such approaches are not primarily concerned with complicity critique serving as a tool for social change nor can they account for white complicity which presumes a subject that is implicated in unjust structures, even if one is not singularly responsible for those structures.

A third distinctive feature of white complicity follows from those who understand white complicity as a way of being. Sara Ahmed[36] describes whiteness as an orientation to the world. Similarly, Marilyn Frye refers to whiteliness as "a deeply ingrained way of being in the world."[37] According to Frye, whitely people

> consider themselves to be benevolent and good-willed, fair honest and ethical. The judge, preacher, peacemaker, martyr, socialist, professional, moral majority, liberal, radical, conservative, working men and women—nobody admits to being prejudiced, everybody has earned every cent they ever had, doesn't take sides, doesn't hate anybody, and always votes for the person they think best qualified for the job, regardless of the candidate's race, sex, religion or national origin, maybe even regardless of their sexual preferences.[38]

Resonating with this perspective, Shannon Sullivan crucially explains how white ways of being, or as she puts it, unconscious habits, are linked to white privilege through the ability of white people do things, and say things, "without thinking."[39] Identifying attitudes, behaviors, and practices as unconscious habits that are deeply ingrained both in individuals and in the broader society alike provides an explanation for why these are so difficult to unsettle.

It is worth noting that, for Sullivan, good intentions often obscure complicity in systemic racial injustice. For instance, Sullivan offers an illustration of the unconscious habits of "good liberal whites." Such good whites believe that integrating into Black neighborhoods is an ethical and antiracist good and so they move into such neighborhoods. Sullivan, however, reveals (reveals more often to white people) how the idea of white people integrating Black neighborhoods entails "white ontological expansiveness" or the tendency for white people

> to act and think as if all spaces—whether geographical, psychical, linguistic, economic, spiritual, bodily, or otherwise—are or should be available for them to move in and out of as they wish.[40]

Because Sullivan describes ontological expansiveness as a habit of white privilege, an ingrained disposition that often exists beyond the realm of consciousness, this theoretical concept is useful for illustrating how good white intentions can hide a type of arrogant white privilege that ignores the perspective or the agency of marginalized groups.

Finally, white complicity foregrounds the ways in which all white people, regardless of their good intentions, are complicit in the perpetuation of systemic white supremacy. Building on the work of Foucault[41] and Butler,[42] I have previously argued that white people cannot transcend the discourses that constitute them. If white people cannot move outside of the ways in which whiteness works through us, then a stance of vigilant critique is called for. Such a stance can seek out and interrogate "fissures where new possibilities emerge"[43] without assuming transcendence. In other words, all white people have a responsibility to examine the ways in which they are complicit in the maintenance of white supremacy, and then *to act from the basis of that knowledge*. White complicity, thus, brings to our attention the ways in which through the defensive, discursive practices of whiteness and by benefiting from the comfort of white privilege, white people are complicit, whether unwittingly or not, in maintaining the system of racial injustice.

The claim that all white people are complicit (the white complicity claim) has been hotly contested and vehemently denied by white people who believe they are not racist. When I speak about this claim whether in class or at a conference, I am often accosted with the rejoinder, "but not all white people are racist." One way to respond would be to demonstrate how the utterance itself is a reenactment of white privilege, which invites another charge of circular logic. John McWhorter, as well as others, maintains that the claim that all whites are racist "has white Americans muzzled, straitjacketed, tied down, and chloroformed for good measure."[44] Although he is specifically targeting the work of Robin DiAngelo,[45] McWhorter also critiques the white complicity claim which he contends silences white people because, according to him, anything one says is interpreted as racist.

In response to the charge of such intractable circularity, that is, that white people cannot be rid of their complicity, Alison Bailey questions why the objection always gets framed as a binary between acknowledging white complicity and silence. In responding to the circularity charge, I often ask my critic to contemplate what the claim allows one to consider and what the denial of the claim allows one to ignore. In the spirit of Yancy's insistence that in entreating white people to acknowledge how they are implicated in systemic white supremacy he is only trying to help white people see through another lens, I emphasize that the claim all whites are complicit in racism aims not to condemn white people (a constituency of which I am a part) but rather to draw attention to the way power works through individual subjects and groups and that white people cannot transcend the system within which they are constituted.

This does not entail that there is nothing white people can do or say but instead underscores the vigilant critique necessary to recognize the effects of white practices on racially marginalized groups. It means that good intentions will not absolve white individuals of complicity in unjust racist structures because the effects of good intentions, as shall be explored later in this chapter and in the next chapter, can be harmful. More than this, vigilant critique can make new opportunities possible, an idea intimated when Shannon Sullivan contends,

> The inevitability of white screw-ups with regard to raced and racist situations means to me that white people can stop focusing more or less solely on themselves—what is the impact on me and my moral standing if I do or do not do X in this situation?—and spend more energy figuring out the situation and what might be done to improve it.[46]

Accepting that there is no transcendence for white people unfolds the possibility that one can shift attention away from defending one's innocence and toward how to work in coalitions to dismantle an unjust racial system.

White distancing strategies and white denials of complicity are available discursive moves that allow white people to believe that through their good intentions they transcend racism, they are "good whites." The ways in which this occurs through defenses of white innocence and protections of white ignorance will be discussed in more detail in the next chapter. I turn first to the research involving these white discursive moves here because one way to understand how acknowledging white complicity facilitates perceiving our social world differently is to examine white discourses of denials with an emphasis on their effects for the racially marginalized.

When one assumes that one can transcend whiteness, one can ignore the *consequences* of distancing strategies and white denials of complicity. While there are Black academics and intellectuals, like McWhorter, who maintain that these consequences are inconsequential and that experiences like microaggressions are oversensitively trivial, so much has been written by critical race theorists and Black feminists about the systemic violence that contributes to the material, psychological, and symbolic harms that people of color experience daily. In fact, this experience has been studied under the concept of racial battle fatigue.

Racial battle fatigue, the ubiquitous "physiological, psychological and behavioral strain exacted on racially marginalized and stigmatized groups and the amount of energy they expend coping with and fighting against racism,"[47] has become the pervasively quotidian experience of faculty, students, and staff of color on predominantly white university campuses. Research studying the experiences of students of color who endure microaggressions makes it abundantly clear that racial battle fatigue is not only a product of blatantly obvious insults and invectives but of the cumulative and subtle assaults that are both unrelenting and, also, ambiguous, and thus difficult to name and confirm for those who do not experience such indignities. The resulting emotional turmoil, frustrations, anger, and other serious physical and psychological consequences that affect the lives of students of color and their educational experience have been well-documented.[48] In subsequent chapters, I will build on this claim providing additional layers of the harms one can ignore when the white complicity claim is denied.

WHITE DENIALS OF COMPLICITY AND THEIR EFFECTS

A burgeoning body of research has developed around white denials of complicity in the classroom.[49] Such denials involve discursive ways in which white students reject having any role to play in maintaining systemic racism and in which white students proclaim their white innocence. Kim Case and Annette Hemmings[50] refer to "distancing strategies" to describe how white women preservice teachers avoid being positioned as racist or implicated in systemic oppression. The authors outline three types of distancing strategies: silence, social disassociation, and separation from responsibility. When their white women preservice teachers would remain silent, Case and Hemmings note, they disengaged from class discussions because they were concerned that they might say something that would be construed as racist. When they dissociated, these students did speak up in class but did so in ways that attempted to convince others that they did not participate in the injustice under discussion. These white preservice teachers also exhibited the strategy of separating from responsibility when they repeatedly found ways to attribute responsibility for racial injustice to anyone but themselves.

An apt exemplification of the distancing strategy of silence appears when George Yancy narrates his experience enrolled in a graduate course on African American Literature. He was disappointed with the superficial ways the white graduate students were responding, or not responding, to the assigned texts *Narratives of the Life of Fredrick Douglas* and *Incidents in the Life of a Slave Girl*. Angry and frustrated, he offers to shake them out of their silence saying,

> I would like to know what the rest of you feel about the white racist behavior of the whites in these texts. Do you feel guilty? And how do you feel about the fact that your own whiteness implicates you in a structural white power system from which you are able to gain so many privileges? How do you understand your whiteness vis-à-vis the whites in the texts?[51]

The white students barely knew how to respond and most continued to remain silent. Such silence allows white students to remain innocent by dodging the necessity of considering how white people, even and especially well-intentioned white people, are implicated in the current reality of systemic white supremacy.

Kathy Hytten and John Warren's outstanding ethnography of the rhetorical moves their white students performed in courses that attempt to teach about systemic oppression and privilege offers many examples of such tactics. Among the types of discursive strategies that Hytten and Warren discuss are remaining silent, evading questions, resorting to the rhetoric of ignoring color, focusing on progress, victim blaming, and focusing on culture rather than race. In a significant point, Hytten and Warren emphasize that these discursive moves are culturally sanctioned discourses of evasion that "were not original—that is, they are already available, already common forms of asserting dominance."[52] Crucially for Hytten and Warren, it is not that white people intend to use these strategies (although they do benefit from them in the sense that white comfort is maintained) yet even when unintended, the effect of these rhetorical strategies is *to obstruct engagement* around uncomfortable conversations.

Along similar lines, Alice McIntyre coined the phrase "white talk" to name discourse that functions to "insulate White people from examining their/our individual and collective role(s) in the perpetuation of racism."[53] In her expansion of McIntyre's work, Alison Bailey[54] argues that white talk functions as a barrier to understanding the problem of whiteness. Bailey explains that white talk is "a predictable set of discursive patterns that white folks habitually deploy when asked directly about the connections between white privilege and institutional racism."[55] Noting the many ways that white talk recenters white comfort, Bailey, following McIntyre, addresses how white talk functions "to derail conversations on race, to dismiss counterarguments, to retreat into silence, to interrupt speakers and topics, and to collude with other whites in creating a 'culture of niceness' that makes it difficult to critique the white world."[56] She explains that white talk is an instance of what Elizabeth Spelman refers to as boomerang discourse, "I talk to you but come right back to myself."[57] Such discursive moves not only recenter the white subject but also allows speakers to perceive themselves as a non-racist self.

Bailey offers an important insight to help recognize white talk when she distinguishes between the literal and the functional meaning of speech. For instance, when a white person utters, "I am not a member of the Aryan Nation," this is not merely a literal and descriptive fact about one's political alliances. Even if the literal meaning of the words is true, that is not the point of asserting this "fact." As Bailey contends, "When asserted in response to the white problem question, the remarks do something else: they are offered as evidence of one's innocence."[58] Bailey demonstrates how distancing strategies like white talk refocus the attention on white people and their feelings while simultaneously allowing white people to continue to "feel as if we are thoughtfully engaging race and racism but . . . from a place of imagined invulnerability, comfort, and safety."[59]

Color-evasiveness or "colorblind" ideology is another common way for white people to dissociate themselves from racism. The consequences of insisting that one does not "see race" and that one treats everyone the same has been well-documented.[60] Recall appeals to universal humanity underlying the response "all lives matter" in discussions of the Black Lives Matter Movement. Using Bailey's distinction between literal and functional meanings of speech, it is not that the rejoinder "all lives matter" is untrue or that it does not stem from good intentions. The utterance's literal sense is beside the point because the effect of that utterance is to ignore those "who have to insist they matter to matter."[61] The consequence, thus, is that the utterance diverts attention away from the fact that Black people have been excluded from the idea of "all lives" and the utterance provides a way for white people to continue to convince themselves that they do not contribute to racism because they have good intentions. When white people protect their innocence, however, they forgo the possibility of considering their complicity in racism thereby reifying the very structures they allege to oppose. "Colorblindness" maintains systemic racism without appearing racist, what Bonilla-Silva refers to as "racism without racists." In other words, one does not have to change what one does not have to name.

While the ontological, moral, and epistemic payoffs of white talk for white people have been given much attention in the scholarship and will also be discussed in upcoming chapters, including the ways that white talk protects white innocence and closes off alternative ways of knowing, I want to briefly stress the harms that people of color endure when they are subjected to white talk.

When students of color, for instance, sit through uninterrupted white talk in class discussions, they often face a dilemma. Do they attempt to educate white students about how such discourse dismisses and diverts attention from the lived experience of racially marginalized students or do they retreat by remaining silent? Students of color live in a catch-22 whereby they must either uphold the comfort of whites who spend their psychic energy trying to "prove" their innocence or speak up insisting on a space of integrity. Both have oppressive consequences. If they choose to educate and get frustrated or angry when white students continue to use white talk, then racially marginalized students also risk being dismissed and labeled as "angry." If they remain silent, they will likely have to endure listening to how white students defend their "good intentions" that, again, recenters white needs and interests and marginalizes their needs. This can be exhausting and often leads to "racial battle fatigue," described earlier, especially when racially marginalized students attempt to use their experiences to prove the realities of structural oppression to white students but receive no serious uptake.

In her book entitled *On Being Included*, Sara Ahmed,[62] a Black feminist scholar, explains how the "hearing" of antiracist critique as an accusation is a "subtle but effective" strategy used by white people to reframe the subject of the critique to be the white victim. As she points out, "the two words 'racism' and 'accusation,' when stuck together, tend to conjure up a scene of an individual subject who is under attack by a collective."[63] Thus, white reality and white emotional comfort are prioritized over the experiences of racism that people of color endure. In subsequent chapters, the *epistemic* harms to the racially marginalized will be further addressed and in more detail.

I close this section with an argument brought forward by Matt Whitt[64] to remind us that white talk and distancing strategies do more than just deny complicity in racial injustice but also "perpetuate socially sanctioned forms of ignorance that misconstrue not only particular injustices, but also the social positions, power relations, and ways of knowing shaped by those injustices."[65] In other words, the benefits of white talk and distancing strategies for white people is not simply that their self-image as "good" is preserved but also that the consequences of such discursive moves protect white ways of perceiving that are comfortable. In chapter 2, I build on Whitt's argument to demonstrate the ways in which white denials of complicity that protect white innocence are intertwined with the preservation of willful ignorance.

A noteworthy point in Whitt's account is that he asks us as educators to reflect on how we, too, use distancing strategies in the classroom.

> It is worthwhile for us to reflect on the diversions, short- cuts, and easy outs we may have taken, in class discussions and syllabus construction, to distance ourselves from systemic injustices and unearned privilege. In conversations with students, I have caught myself thinking "Why did I say it like that?" after emphasizing my own very minor role on the right side of a social justice issue.[66]

My aim in this book is likewise to turn attention to the white educator and to how acknowledging complicity complicates pedagogy.

Feminist critical race scholars Fellows and Razack[67] advocate that white people shift their focus away from innocence and toward complicity. As this chapter has shown, acknowledging complicity is not about blame or guilt but about developing an understanding of how we are positioned within oppressive structures so that we can work together with others to disrupt those structures. The white complicity claim aims not to silence white people but to help white people understand that the assertion of innocence is not innocent.

CHAPTER SUMMARIES

In chapter 2, I examine how white denials of complicity function to preserve white innocence and protect white ignorance. I argue that there is an interrelationship between the former and the latter. The role of good intentions, whether alleged or sincere, in obscuring the effects of white discursive moves are addressed through a review of the critiques of whiteness within feminism. A primary way that whiteness is maintained in feminism is through the construction of white feminists as innocent subjects. The chapter also explores the meaning and effects of systemic white ignorance and willful ignorance. The aim of the chapter is to make explicit how desires for white innocence function as a fundamental force in preserving white ignorance and maintaining epistemic injustice.

Chapter 3 critically examines some of the remedies recommended to combat epistemic injustice. Traditional scholarship often focuses on two aspects of humility: an avoidance of arrogance and owning one's limitations. When humility is advanced as a tool that white individuals should cultivate to disrupt white innocence and for unsettling white ignorance, a richer notion of humility is required. The call for humility is developed further through an exploration of Alison Bailey's notion of humility grounded in vulnerability, through the critique of Miranda Fricker's call for sensitivity to bias, and through a discussion of Jose Medina's work on epistemic friction. Since open-mindedness is often discussed as a characteristic of humility, the recent scholarship on open-mindedness is examined. Finally, a vigilantly vulnerable informed humility is introduced as a means of combating the white innocence and white ignorance that protects epistemic injustice from challenges.

Chapter 4 critically examines three pedagogical challenges that white educators who teach about whiteness to a racially diverse group of students encounter. Insights from the previous chapters will be drawn forth to suggest ways to address these challenges. The three challenges addressed in this chapter are related. The first challenge critically addresses a common pedagogical assumption: teach students "where they are at." One consequence of white educators teaching white students "where they are at" entails *a hesitancy to challenge them* when they reproduce whiteness in subtle ways that are not visible to them yet. Yet what is considered subtle reproduction of whiteness for white students and educators is often exceedingly obvious to students of color.

This leads to a second challenge that white educators may encounter related to an ambiguity experienced by the white educator around white students' learning and the violence it generates in the classroom. When white educators are uncertain about or have a difficulty with the distinction between the literal interpretation of an utterance and what such an utterance does (its impact), they, as in the previous case, might hesitate to call out white students' discursive reproduction of whiteness in the classroom.

Hesitating to critically challenge white students again segues into a third challenge. There are many studies that show white educators hesitate or refuse to challenge students of color and, thereby, possibly denying them critical feedback that they need to progress through their academic program.

This chapter attempts to connect the bodies of scholarship in critical whiteness studies and epistemic injustice with the experiences of some white educators in the hopes that the insights from the scholarship can help white educators support more meaningful learning for all their students. The chapter also aims to further illuminate what a vigilantly vulnerable informed humility can mean.

Finally, chapter 5 concludes the book by offering two suggestions that may be crucial for the cultivation of vigilantly vulnerable informed humility—being willing to rock the boat and developing white double consciousness.

NOTES

1. George Yancy, "Dear White America." *The New York Times* (December 24, 2015).
2. Ibid.
3. Ibid.
4. George Yancy, *Backlash: What Happens When We Talk Honestly about Racism in America* (Lanham, MD: Rowman & Littlefield, 2018).
5. Ibid., 66.
6. Clearly, "white" and "people of color" do not refer to homogenous or essentialized identity categories and that whiteness is multifaceted and intersects with gender, sexuality, ablism, and other social positionalities and identities. Systemically oppressed and systemically privileged positionalities can intersect in the same person. Moreover, while the racial binary is problematically flawed, I focus on whiteness as a first step to making explicit the dynamics of systemic white supremacy to those who do not have to consider its effects. In addition, Black and other racially marginalized groups are capitalized as a form of linguistic empowerment. The term "white" will not be capitalized to counter its linguistic power.
7. See David R. Roediger, ed., *Black Writers on What It Means to Be White* (New York: Schocken Books, 1998); Charles W. Mills, "White Right: The Idea of a Herrenvolk Ethics," in his *Blackness Visible: Essays on Philosophy and Race* (Ithaca, NY: Cornell University Press, 1998): 139–166; W.E.B. Du Bois, *The Souls of Black Folk* (Boston, MA: Bedford Books, 1920); bell hooks, *Black Looks: Race and Representation* (Boston, MA: South End Press, 1992); Langston Hughes, *The Ways of White Folk* (New York: A.A. Knopf, 1969); and Toni Morrison, *Playing in the Dark: Whiteness and the Literary Imagination* (New York: Vintage Books, 1992).

8. Audre Lorde, "The Master's Tools will Never Dismantle the Master's House," in her *Sister Outsider: Essays and Speeches* (Berkeley, CA: Crossing Press, 1984): 110–114; bell hooks, "Racism and Feminism." *Ain't I a Woman: Black Women and Feminism* (Second Edition) (New York: Routledge, 2015); Marilyn Frye, *The Politics of Reality: Essays in Feminist Theory* (New York: Crossing Press, 1983): Mary Louise Fellows and Sherene Razack, "The Race to Innocence: Confronting Hierarchical Relations Among Women." *Journal of Gender, Race and Justice* 1 (1998): 335–52; Aileen Moreton-Robinson, *Talkin' Up to the White Woman: Indigenous Women and Feminism* (Queensland: University of Queensland Press, 2000); María Lugones, *Pilgrimages Peregrinajes: Theorizing Coalition Against Multiple Oppressions* (Lanham, MD: Rowman & Littlefield, 2003); Sara Ahmed, "Declarations of Whiteness: The Non-Performativity of Anti- Racism." *Borderlands* 3, no. 2 (2004), www.borderlands.net.au/vol3no2_2004/ ahmed_declarations.htm; Sarita Srivastava, "'You're Calling Me a Racist?' The Moral and Emotional Regulation of Antiracism and Feminism." *Signs: Journal of Women in Culture and Society* 31, no. 1 (2005): 29–62; Mariana Ortega, "Being Lovingly, Knowingly Ignorant: White Feminism and Women of Color." *Hypatia* 21, no. 3 (2006): 56–74; Gloria Wekker, *White Innocence: Paradoxes of Colonialism and Race* (London: Duke University Press, 2017); Terese Jonsson, *Innocent Subjects: Feminism and Whiteness* (Pluto Press, 2021).

9. Mark Sanders, *Complicities: The Intellectual and Apartheid* (Indiana: Duke University Press, 2002).

10. David Roediger, *The Wages of Whiteness: Race and the Making of the American Working Class* (New York and London: Verso. 1991).

11. Ruth Frankenberg, *White Women, Race Matters: The Social Construction of Whiteness* (Minneapolis, MN: University of Minnesota Press, 1993): 1.

12. Cheryl Harris, "Whiteness as Property," *Harvard Law Review* 106, no. 8 (1993): 1707–1791.

13. Jonathan Warren and France Winddance Twine, "White Americans, the New Minority? Non-Blacks and the Ever-Expanding Boundaries of Whiteness." *Journal of Black Studies* 28, no. 2 (1997): 215.

14. George Yancy, *Backlash*, 74-75.

15. Charles Mills, "White Supremacy as Sociopolitical System: A Philosophical Perspective." In Ashley "Woody" Doane and Eduardo Bonilla-Silva, eds. *White Out: The Continuing Significance of Racism* (New York: Routledge, 2003): 35–48.

16. Frances Lee Ansely, "Stirring the Ashes: Race, Class and the Future of Civil Rights Scholarship." *Cornell Law Review* 74 (1989): note 129 on page 1024.

17. David Gillborn, "Rethinking White Supremacy: Who Counts in 'White World'?" *Ethnicities* 6, no. 3 (2006): 318.

18. Audrey Thompson, "Tiffany, Friend of People of Color: White Investments in Antiracism." *International Journal of Qualitative Studies in Education* 16, no. 1 (2003): 7.

19. Ibid.

20. Ibid.

21. Throughout the book, when I reference white educators, I often shift from first-person to third-person, although I am a white educator. I include myself in everything I write about white educators in the book. The shift is only for ease of writing style.

22. Kristie Dotson, "A Cautionary Tale: On Limiting Epistemic Oppression." *Frontiers: A Journal of Women Studies* 33, no. 1 (2012): 24.

23. Fiona Probyn-Rapsey, "Complicity, Critique, and Methodology." *Ariel* 38, no. 2–3 (2007): 65–82; Fiona Probyn, "Playing Chicken at the Intersection: The White Critic in/of Critical Whiteness Studies." *Borderlands* 13, no.2 (2004). http://www.borderlandsejournal.adelaide.edu.au/vol3no2_2004/probyn_playing.htm

24. Barbara Applebaum, *Being White, Being Good: White Complicity, White Moral Responsibility, and Social Justice Pedagogy* (Lanham, MD: Lexington Books, 2020): 147.

25. Julia Daniels and Heather Hebard, "Complicity, Responsibility, and Authorization: A Praxis of Critical Questioning for White Literacy Educators." *English Teaching: Practice and Critique* 17, no 1 (2018): 16–27.

26. Ibid., 17.

27. Ibid., 20–23.

28. Zak Foste, "Remaining Vigilant: Reflexive Considerations for White Researchers Studying Whiteness." *Whiteness and Education* 5, no. 3 (2020): 1–16.

29. Ibid., 1.

30. Christopher Kutz, *Complicity: Ethics and Law for a Collective Age* (Cambridge: Cambridge University Press, 2000).

31. Giuliana Monteverde, "Navigating Complicity in Contemporary Feminist Discourse." In Afxentis Afxentiou, Robin Dunford and Michael Neu, eds. *Exploring Complicity: Concept, Cases and Critique* (New York: Rowman & Littlefield, 2017): 99.

32. Mark Sanders, *Complicities*.

33. George Yancy, *Black Bodies, White Gazes: The Continuing Significance of Race* (Lanham, Maryland: Lexington, 2008): 2.

34. Afexentis Afxentious et al., "Introducing Complicity." In their edited volume, *Exploring Complicity*, 1–17.

35. Owen Thomas, "Blind to Complicity? Official Truth and the Hidden Role of Methods." In *Exploring Complicity*, 162. Also see George Yancy and Todd May, "Policing is Doing What It was Meant to Do. That's the Problem." *New York Times*, June 21, 2020.

36. Sara Ahmed, "The Phenomenology of Whiteness." *Feminist Theory* 8, no. 2 (2007): 149–168.

37. Marilyn Frye, "White Woman Feminist," in her *Willful Virgin: Essays in Feminism 1976–1992* (Freedom, CA: Crossing Press): 151.

38. Ibid., 154.

39. Shannon Sullivan, *Revealing Whiteness: The Unconscious Habits of Racial Privilege* (Bloomington, IN: Indiana University Press, 2006): 4.

40. Ibid., 10.

41. Michel Foucault, *The History of Sexuality Vol. 2* (New York: Vintage Books, 1985).

42. Judith Butler, "Explanation and Exoneration, or What We Can Hear." *Social Text* 72, 20, no. 3 (2002): 177–188; Judith Butler, *Precarious Life: The Powers of Mourning and Violence* (New York: Verso, 2004).

43. Barbara Applebaum, *Being White, Being Good,* 191.

44. John McWhorter, "The Dehumanizing Condescension of White Fragility." *The Atlantic*, July 15, 2020.

45. Robin DiAngelo, *White Fragility: Why It's So Hard for White People to Talk about Racism* (Boston, MA: Beacon Press, 2018).

46. Shannon Sullivan, *Revealing Whiteness*, 234.

47. William A. Smith, "Higher Education: Racial Battle Fatigue," in *Encyclopedia of Race, Ethnicity, and Society*, ed. R. T. Schaefer (Thousand Oaks, CA: Sage, 2008): 617.

48. Willian A. Smith, Tara Yosso, and David Solorzano, "Challenging Racial Battle Fatigue on Historically White Campuses: A Critical Race Examination of Race-related Stress." In *Faculty of Color Teaching in Predominantly White Colleges and Universities*, ed. C. A. Stanley (Bolton, MA: Anker, 2006): 299–327.

49. Estella Williams Chizhik and Alexander Williams Chizhik, "Are you Privileged or Oppressed? Students' Conceptions of Themselves and Others" *Urban Education* 40, no. 2 (2005): 116–143; Rudolfo Chavez Chavez and James O'Donnell, *Speaking the Unpleasant: The Politics of (non)Engagement in the Multicultural Education Terrain* (Albany, NY: State University Press, 1998); Ann Berlak, "Teaching and Testimony: Witnessing and Bearing Witness to Racisms in Culturally Diverse Classrooms." *Curriculum Inquiry* 29, no. 1 (1999): 99–127; Audrey Thompson, "Entertaining Doubts: Enjoyment and Ambiguity in White, Antiracist Classrooms." In *Passion and Pedagogy: Relation, Creation, and Transformation in Teaching,* ed. Elijah Mirochick and Debora C. Sherman (New York: Peter Lang, 2002): 431–452; Leslie G. Roman, "White is a Color! White Defensiveness, Postmodernism and Anti-racist Pedagogy." In *Race, Identity and Representation in Education,* ed. Cameron McCarthy and Warren Crinchlow (New York: Routledge, 1993): 71–88; Bonnie TuSmith, "Out on a Limb: Race and the Evaluation of Frontline Teaching." In *Race in the College Classroom*, ed. Bonnie TuSmith and Maureen T. Reddy (New Brunswick, NJ: Rutgers University Press, 2002): 112–125.

50. Kim Case and Annette Hemmings, "Distancing: White Women Preservice Teachers and Antiracist Curriculum," *Urban Education* 40, no. 6 (2005): 606–626.

51. George Yancy, *Black Bodies, White Gazes,* 42.

52. Kathy Hytten and John Warren, "Engaging Whiteness: How Racial Power Gets Reified in Education." *Qualitative Studies in Education* 16, no. 1 (2003): 66.

53. Alice McIntyre, *Making Meaning of Whiteness: Exploring Racial Identity with White Teachers* (Albany, NY: State University of New York Press, 1997): 45.

54. Alison Bailey, "'White Talk' as a Barrier to Understanding Whiteness." In George Yancy (ed.), *White Self-Criticality beyond Anti-racism: How Does It Feel to Be a White Problem?* (Lanham, MD: Lexington Books, 2014): 37–57.

55. Ibid., 38.

56. Ibid., 41.

57. Elizabeth Spelman, *Inessential Woman: Problems of Exclusion in Feminist Thought* (Boston, MA: Beacon Press, 1988): 12.
58. Alison Bailey, "White Talk as a Barrier," 44.
59. Ibid., 43.
60. Eduardo Bonilla-Silva, *Racism without Racists: Color-Blind Racism and the Persistence of Racial Inequality in America* (New York: Rowman & Littlefield, 2017).
61. Sara Ahmed, https://feministkilljoys.com/2014/08/25/selfcare-as-warfare/
62. Sara Ahmed, *On Being Included: Racism and Diversity in Institutional Life* (Durham, NC: Duke University Press, 2012).
63. Ibid., 210, n. 8.
64. Matt Whitt, "Other People's Problems: Student Distancing, Epistemic Responsibility, and Injustice." *Studies in Philosophy of Education* 35 (2016): 427–444.
65. Ibid., 431.
66. Ibid., 434.
67. Mary Louise Fellows and Sherene Razack, "The Race to Innocence."

Chapter 2

The Entangled Armor of White Complicity

Innocence and Ignorance

PROTECTING INNOCENCE, PRESERVING IGNORANCE

I open this chapter returning to the appeal George Yancy makes to white American, already noted in chapter 1, in which he exhorts white people to stop protecting their innocence. As Yancy attempts to prod white people to take responsibility for their whiteness, he writes,

> If you are white, and you are reading this letter, I ask that you don't run to seek shelter from your own racism. Don't hide from your responsibility. . . . After all, it is painful to let go of your "white innocence," to use this letter as a mirror, one that refuses to show you what you want to see, one that demands that you look at the lies that you tell yourself so that you don't feel the weight of responsibility for those who live under the yoke of whiteness, your whiteness.[1]

This chapter builds on Yancy's counsels arguing how protecting innocence contributes to the preservation of ignorance.

In chapter 1, the scholarship around the various defensive, discursive moves available to white individuals that sanction whites' ability to evade acknowledgment of complicity in systemic white supremacy was discussed. Noting the effects of these white discursive moves on the lived reality of the racially marginalized reveals the ways in which these discursive moves themselves are indications of complicity and effectively shield white individuals from accountability. In this chapter, the role that desires for white innocence and protections of white ignorance play in white complicity is addressed in more detail.

The first section examines the role of good intentions, whether alleged or sincere, in obscuring the effects of white discursive moves. More significantly, this section aims to make explicit how desires for white innocence function as a fundamental force in preserving white ignorance. While white innocence has been addressed in some legal writings as briefly noted in this chapter, a significant site for examining white innocence and its harmful effects can be found in the critiques by feminists of color who expose the persistence of whiteness as a normative and recentering framework within much past and contemporary feminist theorizing and activism. A primary way that whiteness is maintained in feminism is through the construction of white feminists as innocent subjects.[2]

In the second section, the meaning and effects of systemic white ignorance and willful ignorance will be explored. The third section focuses on the insights this scholarship can offer to white educators who teach white students about whiteness. The final section spotlights how this scholarship can guide white educators who teach about whiteness in their attempts to better attend to the needs of their students of color.

WHITE INNOCENCE

In a 1990 article, Thomas Ross[3] addresses white innocence from a legal perspective and exposes how the rhetoric around the innocence of white individuals relationally constitutes people of color as guilty perpetrators. White innocence is defined by Ross as "the insistence on the innocence or absence of responsibility of the contemporary white person."[4] He demonstrates that throughout the legal history of the United States, white people have been assured that they will not be considered guilty of a crime simply because of their skin color. The same presumption of innocence is not afforded to the racially marginalized who are often *characteristically* considered guilty as evidenced by the systemic violence they experience from the police, discriminatory law enforcement, and mass incarceration. Ross critically investigates the rhetorical moves of implicit bias that presume white innocence and Black guilt.

Resonating with Yancy's contention that race is relational, as discussed in chapter 1, Ross adds that the representation of people of color as guilty perpetrators is coconstructed through white innocence and this construction operates through "abstraction." As an illustration of what he means by abstraction, Ross offers that in the 1954 U.S. Supreme Court case, *Brown v Board of Education*, John W. Davis, the lead attorney for the defense of segregation, argued that the happiness, progress, and welfare of Black children "is best promoted in segregated schools,"[5] a claim that would only make sense if the presence of racism as the context for segregated schools is abstracted. Ross argues that only by ignoring the context of racism can the relationality of race can be ignored. Consequently, the humanity of Black children can be denied, and their daily experiences negated.

The term "innocence" comprises several meanings. First, as narrowly defined, innocence refers to being not legally guilty of a crime or offense. Yet, there is a broader concept of innocence that denotes "freedom from sin, guilt, or moral wrong in general; the state of being untainted with, or unacquainted with evil; moral purity."[6] Consequently, someone who is naïve, unaware, or weak and vulnerable can also be examples of innocence. As Cecil Hunt II[7] reminds us, the concept of innocence is often used to evoke the untainted infant who is pure in thought and deed and, thus, commands the care and protection from harm of others.

White innocence in the way I use it in this book signals a presumed transcendence of whiteness in three senses. First, the premise of white innocence gestures to the privilege that white people have to ignore their racial positionality. In other words, white innocence means that one can be ignorant of (in the sense of being able to ignore) one's white racial perspective or positionality, as if white racial perspective is a race-neutral perspective rather than a particular and exclusionary perspective. This understanding of white innocence feeds into color-evasive[8] ideology that hides a dominant white perspective under the veneer of normalcy. Second and relatedly, white innocence indicates that white people can consider themselves as uninvolved and unimplicated in the legacy of American racism. Racism, under the ideology of white innocence, is not a white problem because racism happens somewhere else—that is, it is not about me! White people can believe that they are not only not racist but also can deny any implication in the racism that they impute elsewhere. White innocence highlights how white people can continue to benefit, as if innocently, from the unjust racial system that they actively have a role in maintaining. Finally, white innocence manifests in prioritizing of white needs, feelings, and interests (a recentering) while simultaneously excluding and marginalizing the racial reality of people of color and then mystifying this process so that it does not seem as if this is happening. Recentering white needs, feelings, and interests is one of the elemental manifestations of white complicity, as will become evident.

The *effects* of white innocence are often obscured by good intentions. Richard Orozco and Jesus Jaime Diaz[9] reveal how altruistic rhetoric in schools that invokes white innocence eclipses the ineffective and oppressive experiences of students of color and reifies white supremacist practices and policies. In a transnational context, Gloria Wekker[10] examines the paradoxical ways in which the Dutch can see themselves as "good" while simultaneously enacting racist discourses and practices that ignore their colonial past. Wekker describes how the white Dutch self-image as a "just, ethical nation; color-blind, thus free of racism; as being inherently on the moral and ethical high ground, thus a guiding light to other folks and nations"[11] inconsistently exists alongside an erasure of the colonial history of imperialism that neutralizes whiteness and allows the Dutch to ignore the contemporary abhorrence of multiculturalism masked in discourse which refuses to name racism. Perceiving themselves as having good intentions blocks the ability of the Dutch to acknowledge their past and present entanglements with racism. This active inattention, then again, serves to protect the moral superiority and moral purity through a denial of the significance of race and an unwillingness to acknowledge the terrorizing effects of whiteness on the lived realities of the racially marginalized. By conserving innocence, Dutch society also preserve ignorance, an idea that will be advanced later in this chapter.

One of the manifestations of white innocence is color-evasiveness. In her 1993 book *White Women, Race Matters*, white feminist sociologist Ruth Frankenberg sets out to theoretically study the meanings that white women ascribe to race. By categorizing and naming the various "discursive repertoires" employed by her informants, Frankenberg captures the fluid ways that white women relate to their whiteness. One of Frankenberg's findings involves the unmarked nature of whiteness for most of the women she interviewed. Frankenberg refers to these discursive habits as "color-evasiveness," or the claim not to see race in others as well as in oneself. These white women sought to focus on similarities between women and ignored any racially different markers. Yet by avoiding difference, white women were able to ignore the power that is unequally distributed among women and, consequently, they were able to see themselves as powerless victims who are "good." By disregarding their white power and privilege, white women were able to retain their image as innocent. Frankenberg also identified white women employing "race-cognizant" repertoires, that is, women who acknowledged the significance of race and racism. Whether the women used evasive or cognizant discourse, it was clear to Frankenberg that addressing race challenged the status of the innocence of the white subject.

In her study of white-centered British feminism, Terese Jonsson similarly shows how even as feminist theory vacillates between color-power evasiveness, on the one hand, and race-cognizant framings, on the other, it is still white innocence that obstructs the possibility of decentering whiteness in feminism. In other words, Jonsson maintains that white feminists who are admittedly committed to progressive politics still have an intense investment in being "good." White-centered feminism, according to Jonsson, is upheld by white innocence. Jonsson explicitly utilizes the term "white-centered feminism" instead of "white feminism" to acknowledge that many white feminists today acknowledge their positionality and understand the dangers of essentializing feminism from a white perspective. Using the term "white-centered feminism" nevertheless recognizes that whiteness continues to persist as the normative framework within much of contemporary feminist thinking and activism.

White feminists' deep investment in being good is explored by Mary Louise Fellows and Sherene Razack.[12] Fellows and Razack describe a "race to innocence" on the part of white feminists that is grounded in "a deeply felt belief that each of us, as women, is not implicated in the subordination of other women."[13] Drawing attention to how debates in feminism about inequalities between women veer into contentious discussion where white women insist that they are oppressed, therefore innocent, Fellows and Razack underscore how white feminists are not willing to consider the ways in which they may also be oppressors. White women tend to make claims of white exceptionalism, that is, they are the "good" and not the "bad" whites because they are also women and, thus, are also victims who cannot be implicated in the oppression of other women.

When white women abstract race from gender, it becomes possible for them to ensure their own status as innocent. Fellows and Razack maintain that desires for innocence are not detached from the historically gendered construction of the respectable white middle-class woman who is constituted through the othering of non-white women whom white women exploit. Concluding their article, Fellows and Razack suggest that white feminists begin the process of feeling less innocent if they want to contribute to social change. To begin to feel less innocent, they recommend that white feminists constantly reflect on the following questions:

> Where have we positioned other women within our strategies for achieving social justice?
> What do we gain from this positioning?
> How are we implicated in structures of dominance?[14]

I return to this idea of "feeling less innocent" at the conclusion of this chapter.

White innocence is also grounded in ostensibly benevolent intentions that can thwart acknowledgment of complicity through shutting down critical analyses of racial oppression. In her study of women's organizations, Sarita Srivastava[15] recounts how women of color raised concerns about racism at a Toronto shelter for battered women. June Callwood, a prominent white Canadian philanthropist who was also chair of the women's shelter board, reproached the women of color for complaining about racism when they had received so much aid from the shelter. The invocation of "help" is an appeal to innocence—how can you say we are complicit in racism when we helped you? Notably, the mentioning of the assistance women of color received requires a return of gratitude which, subsequently, serves to curtail discussions about racism and white complicity at the shelter.

Since benevolence is considered good, the innocence of the one who bestows benevolence is secured and any implication one might have in perpetuating social injustice can be ignored. The reminder of the good white women who help women of color brought any discussion about the racism existing at the shelter to an end. Remaining focused on the self and preoccupied with one's moral innocence makes seriously considering any broader analyses of racism difficult. Reaffirming concerns with white recentering, Srivastava concludes "that some of the deadlocks of anti-racist efforts are linked to these preoccupations with morality and self."[16]

In the same way, Sara Ahmed[17] demonstrates how appeals to seemingly well-intentioned public declarations of "diversity" and "inclusion" can block critical discussion about the institutional whiteness of a university. In her well-cited ethnographic account of the lived experience of diversity *On Being Included: Racism and Diversity in Institutional Life*, Ahmed interviews twenty-one diversity officers both at Australian and British universities, as well as offering her own insights gleaned from her experiences in similar positions. She finds that institutions rely on "happy diversity talk" to give the illusion that the institution is not racist while simultaneously prohibiting any discussion of prevailing racism by and within the institution. "Diversity" is a happy term, according to Ahmed, a cuddly concept that allows people/institutions to feel good, well not all people—but that is Ahmed's point. Her project calls upon us to question, "What does diversity do?" or, more specifically, "What are we doing when we use the language of diversity?"[18] Her aim is to expose what incantations of diversity obscure.[19]

Focusing on what it means to embody diversity in higher education, Ahmed makes explicit that embodying diversity fulfills a policy commitment. She explains that the body that embodies diversity becomes a performance indicator that allows the institution to believe they have conquered racism. The body that embodies diversity becomes a tick in a box that symbolizes for the institution "the hope or promise that whiteness is being undone."[20] When those who embody diversity speak up about the whiteness of the institution, they are read as ungrateful for the hospitality they have received by virtue of being included. Reminiscent of the way that white "help" that women of color in the shelter received obliged them to be grateful (in Srivastava's study), the bequest of being included in the university also creates implicit expectations of gratitude. On the one hand, inclusion is used as evidence that the institution has overcome institutional whiteness. On the other hand, this welcoming of the "other" is conditional. You are welcomed only so long as you affirm and uphold this good image of the institution where whiteness no longer exists.

Ahmed reveals how diversity is performed as a politics of feeling good, that is *for whites* to feel good and not uncomfortable. To embody diversity is to be under pressure not to "create" bad feelings for whites while the bad feeling that is endured by those who embody diversity is discounted. The very mention of racism is interpreted by whites as introducing bad feelings and is perceived as an attack. Speaking about racism, Ahmed discloses, is "heard as an injury not to those who speak but to those who are spoken about"[21] because it threatens to destroy the "good" reputation of that institution and the fantasy that racism has been overcome.

Reaching out to a figure in feminism that she has previously addressed elsewhere[22]—the feminist killjoy—Ahmed details how this image parallels the lived experience of those who embody diversity at universities. The feminist killjoy exposes the sexism that desires to remain hidden and, thus, she becomes *the* problem. Ahmed provocatively asks us to consider, "Does the feminist kill other people's joy by pointing out moments of sexism? Or does she expose the bad feelings that get hidden, displaced, or negated under public signs of joy?"[23] Ahmed further applies the concept of the feminist killjoy to feminists of color who point to the whiteness of feminism. These feminists of color are then interpolated as the one who is not doing feminism in the "right" way, the one who is threatening the fantasy of warm, fuzzy coziness of feigned solidarity. She goes on to demonstrate how, in white feminism, power is *redone* at the very moment when it is imagined as *undone*.

Similarly, those who embody diversity at the university *become the problem* when *they expose the problem*. According to Ahmed, "The exposure of violence becomes the origin of violence."[24] Like the feminist killjoy who dares to disturb the fantasy of happiness in white-centered feminism and is thus discredited, those who embody diversity unmask the veil of happiness underlying institutional invocations of diversity and inclusion and they bear the consequences. And when those who embody diversity in white institutions express anger at the racism they experience, like the feminist killjoy, they are dismissed with the labeled "the angry person of color." Ahmed describes the process by which one's justified anger gets twisted so that

> your reasonable thoughtful arguments are dismissed as anger (which of course empties anger of its own reason), which makes you angry, such that your response becomes read as the confirmation of the evidence that you are not only angry but also unreasonable.[25]

In other words, as Ahmed so powerfully put it, it is "as if you are against x because you are angry rather than being angry because you are against x."[26] Ahmed[27] emboldens those who embody diversity to stay angry and be willing to rock the boat. "We are willing to rock the boat," Ahmed insists, if "that boat is whiteness."[28]

White tears function as another way to silence justified anger. In 2018, Ruby Hamad wrote an essay that went viral. "How White Women Use Strategic Tears to Silence Women of Color" has since turned into a book, *White Tears/Brown Scars: How White Feminism Betrays Women of Color*,[29] which addresses how white tears serve to uphold innocence and result in scars that wound women of color. Once again attesting to the problem of recentering white feeling, she begins her book by asking, "How is it that we have been so conditioned to privilege the emotional comfort of white people?" When white women hear women of color bring up the topic or racism or whiteness, a common response is to interpret these conversations as a personal attack which ends up with white women crying.

Hamad refers to such tears as "a strategically wielded innocence" because such tears give white women the permission to leave the conversation. More than that, however, she provocatively exposes how white tears demand comfort, absolution, a warm hug. This centering of white women's feelings comes at the expense of the feelings and experiences of women of color. Furthermore, when women of color refuse to console white tears, they are maligned as uncaring.

In her study of women's organizations mentioned earlier, Srivastava similarly draws attention to white women's tearful reactions to antiracist critiques. White defensiveness and denials are often followed by tears that have "moral undertones" implying white women's racial innocence is under siege. This attachment to one's self-image as "good" often leads white women to focus their energies in defending their innocence rather than learning how they can work together with others to challenge systemic white supremacy. In other words, just like invocations of help, white tears serve as a stop-guard ending difficult conversations that might implicate white women in racism. When women of color get justifiably frustrated and angry, white women often tone police and constrain such anger.

Audre Lorde so famously exposes the discourse of white tone policing of women of color. White feminists tell feminists of color, "Tell me how you feel but don't say it too harshly or I cannot hear you."[30] Echoing Lorde, Sara Ahmed also points to the ways that the discourse of happiness and solidarity constrains the ability of women of color to point out racism and heterosexism in feminism. Summoning the trope of the "angry black woman," white feminists accuse women of color of being the cause of feminist unhappiness when their anger, in fact, exposes unjust unhappiness that already exists in enraging forms.

Not only are dismissals of justified anger a form of disrespect, but they also serve to safeguard the innocence of the dominantly situated group. This is most palpable in the ways in which responsibility is shifted away from the one who stands to learn from anger to the one expressing anger. By focusing on the expression of anger and blaming the person who expresses anger, dominantly situated group members can avoid considering how they might have contributed to what caused the anger. This defensiveness relationally positions the one who dismisses anger outside the framework of systemic injustice and consequently protects innocence. Shifting the blame to the other, thus, constitutes one as an innocent subject, as Jonsson so explicitly puts it. It is the comfort and presumed innocence of white women that is prioritized above the legitimate concerns and feelings of women of color.

Although there are many additional ways that the effects of good intentions and the consequences of protecting white innocence reproduce oppression, I turn attention away from the scholarship around white feminism toward educational research that also provides evidence regarding how good white intentions create unjust experiences for the marginalized. This shift will also serve as a segue to the section on ignorance and epistemic injustice.

In her oft-cited critique of the desire for dialogue across difference, Alison Jones[31] reveals that white students' desire to learn about difference, ostensibly considered a refusal to be ignorant, is, ironically, a passion for ignorance. Jones analyzes the students' feedback when in a course on feminist theory, the white (Pakeha) students and the students of color (Maori and Pacific Islander) were divided for a significant part of the course. While the white students were angry and upset, the students of color were energetically overjoyed. Jones reads these different responses as symptomatic of the differential power that exists in racially and ethnically integrated classrooms. What becomes obvious is that when confronted with a denial of access to their marginalized peers, the white students felt resentment stemming from being "displaced from the unproblematic centre of knowing."[32] White students express an entitlement to know the experiences of their marginalized classmates that is couched in a plea for sympathetic assistance, for "compassion and understanding, even love."[33] For Jones, these pleas are understood as calls by white students to indicate that they are not powerful, not threatening, and that they only want to learn, and so, please, "Care for me!"

While the white students demanded to be taught by the marginalized ("How else would we learn?"), the students of color were relieved to have a separate space not only to focus on their own interests but also to evade the violence of experiencing the white students' learning that almost always resorted to skepticism of what the students of color said. One student of color wrote in her journal about the experience of being in the class with the white students, "I prepared myself to argue any point."[34] This mirrors what Maria Lugones and Elizabeth Spelman[35] write,

We have had to be in your world and learn its ways. We have to participate in it, make a living in it, live in it, be mistreated in it, be ignored in it, and rarely, be appreciated in it. In learning to do these things or in learning to suffer them or in learning to enjoy what is to be enjoyed or in learning to understand your conception of us, we have had to learn your culture and thus your language and self-conceptions.[36]

In other words, students of color prepared themselves to defend their knowledge expecting that white students would invalidate them and, instead, recenter white interests, white emotion, and white innocence. As will be addressed in more detail later in the chapter, white students defensively resist what marginally situated knowers tell them and, often, the marginally situated knowers are left to endure a variety of discursive forms of dismissal when they give testimony about their experiences with racism.

Jones's insights about her white students' defensiveness are significant. Her white students simultaneously dismiss what marginalized students tell them while also wanting their marginalized classmates to absolve them from any taint of racism and to assuage white guilt. Leslie Roman[37] refers to white students' desire to know the other as "redemption fantasies" that enable white people to retain their investments in whiteness and their white innocence. This desire is more about a desire *not to know about white complicity* in systemic racial injustice and less about a desire to know about the marginalized other. Jones maintains that the racially integrated classroom habitually recenters white students' needs and feelings. In his celebrated book *The Racial Contract*,[38] Charles Mills uses an aphorism from Black American folklore as an epigraph to his book, "When white people say 'justice,' they mean 'just us.'"

One way that social justice education reinforces whiteness involves the exclusive attention it gives to raising white students' consciousness of their complicity in the perpetuation of white supremacy. A consequence of this focus is that students of color experience a double bind. On the one hand, they are positioned to bear the burden of cross-cultural work and are pressed into teaching white students about racism. On the other hand, they must endure white denials of complicity, white distancing strategies and white talk, as described in chapter 1. In addition, when students of color are willing to explain their experiences with racism, and especially the racism they experience in their classroom, they are dismissed and scorned for disrupting white comfort.

In her discussion of how the quest for redemption ensures that whites will remain the center of social justice education, Deanna Blackwell[39] explains that students of color are expected to serve as "aids" to assist the antiracist educator in penetrating white students' defensiveness as well as to serve as "a confidant and cheerleader" in white students' struggle to become race conscious. White educators often expect students of color to teach. Jones also draws attention to the white educator and how white students' apparent epiphanies offer a site of pleasure to white progressive teachers which might help us understand why white teachers often recenter white students' learning to the detriment of the needs and interests of students of color.

In this section, support was provided for the claim that assertions of innocence are *not* innocent but rather a strategy for maintaining racial power through shielding ignorance from challenges. So long as innocence is tenaciously defended, ignorance will not be interrupted. How do white innocence and white ignorance reciprocally impact the pedagogy of the white educator and social justice pedagogy? To fill in the context in which this question arises, we need first to review some of the recent scholarships on epistemic injustice and willful ignorance.

EPISTEMIC INJUSTICE AND WILLFUL IGNORANCE

In her widely cited book *Epistemic Injustice: Power and the Ethics of Knowing*, Miranda Fricker[40] coins the term "epistemic injustice" to address the ways in which members of marginalized groups are not justly treated as epistemic agents. Fricker maintains that the harms of epistemic injustice exacerbate social harms so that epistemic injustice and social injustice are integrally related,[41] yet there is a distinctively epistemic type of injustice in which someone is wronged specifically in their capacity as a knower. The idea of epistemic injustice highlights the mutual entanglement of ethics and epistemology that earlier trailblazing feminist philosophers pioneered, themselves targets of the very epistemic marginalization that Fricker describes.[42]

Fricker identifies two types of epistemic injustice: testimonial injustice and hermeneutical injustice. Testimonial injustice occurs when "prejudice causes a hearer to give a deflated level of credibility to a speaker's word"[43] or when an individual's expression of knowledge is granted less credibility due to factors such as race, gender, or other markers of marginalized social identity, what today is often referred to as implicit bias. Hermeneutical injustice occurs when the collective hermeneutical resources are shaped by the experiences of dominantly situated knowers so that a lacuna or gap in the collective conceptual resources, according to Fricker, makes it difficult for the marginally situated knower to understand their own experiences.[44] In both cases of testimonial and hermeneutical injustice, the person's capacity as an epistemic agent is jeopardized because one's ability to share knowledge with others is unjustly diminished.

One of the illustrations of testimonial injustice that Fricker provides concerns the trial of Tom Robinson, drawn from Harper Lee's book *To Kill a Mockingbird*,[45] in which the jury does not perceive the testimony of Robinson, a Black man, as credible simply because of his race. Fricker maintains that a credibility deficit based on identity prejudice results in the target being treated as an object in the sense of being denied status as someone who is an agent capable of having an active effect on listeners.

Portending a major limitation of Fricker's project, Gaile Pohlhaus Jr.[46] argues that the point is not only that Robinson is dismissed because of identity prejudice but that his credibility *is selectively affirmed or denied depending on whether it conforms to the dominantly situated knower's framework*. Anything the target might try to express that is beyond dominant epistemic frameworks is unrecognized and not given uptake. Drawing attention to how the jurors continuously misinterpret Tom's words and, thus, fail to appropriately consider the evidence presented at the trial that supported his innocence, Pohlhaus underscores that it is the white jurors' refusal to seriously engage with the epistemic resources that even Tom's lawyer, Atticus Finch, used to explain Tom's words and his world. To do so would threaten their own identity and the dominant epistemic frameworks that uphold their positionality. If the speaker's words challenge dominant frameworks of intelligibility, the hearer either dismisses what is said or reshapes and misinterprets what is said in ways that fit his dominant framework. The speaker's epistemic, agential ability to affect and possibly change what the hearer thinks becomes moot.

Pohlhaus's insight underscores that while testimonial injustice harms the one denied credibility in her capacity as a knower, it also has consequences for the person who denies credibility. Testimonial injustice curtails what one considers. Evidence, opposing ideas, and new concepts that are conducive to knowledge expansion can be ignored. Ignorance is, thus, maintained by testimonial injustice, and such epistemic exclusions result in more general deficiencies in collective social knowledge.

Turning to the consequences to the one whose credibility is dismissed, Kristie Dotson discerns two types of silencing that result from testimonial injustice: testimonial quieting and testimonial smothering.[47] Testimonial quieting occurs when, because of identity prejudice, the hearer does not regard the speaker as a knower or source of knowledge. Because the speaker is not given the appropriate uptake, *it is as if the speaker did not speak at all*. For example, it is not just that Tom Robinson's testimony suffers credibility deficit but, rather, that his testimony means nothing to the jury. If a speaker recognizes that her words are unlikely to receive uptake whether because the hearer is unable or unwilling, she may decide to self-censor or refuse to speak at all. Dotson refers to this as testimonial smothering; the speaker *herself* withholds testimony. Testimonial silencing can lead to testimonial smothering.

As Dotson points out, such self-censoring arises because one anticipates that one's words will not receive uptake, thus, it is a form of *coerced* self-silencing. Testimonial quieting and testimonial smothering often go hand in hand, for when one is consistently refused uptake, self-censoring and withdrawal become a form of self-care and survival.

In her provocatively titled book *Why I'm No Longer Talking to White People About Race*, Reni Eddo-Lodge[48] describes how white people utilize numerous counter-arguments to deny what she says about her experience as a Black woman. Eddo-Lodge declares that she was no longer talking to white people about race since she no longer wants to engage with the emotional disconnect displayed by white people when she attempts to articulate her experience. Withdrawing from hostile spaces is a way to enact her sense of agency and is an understandable way to survive a toxic environment. As we will underscore in chapter 4, it can also be a form of resistance.

A similar decision to disengage is evident in the example Dotson offers to illustrate epistemic smothering. Dotson refers to a 1996 article by Cassandra Byers Harvin[49] titled "Conversations I Can't Have," in which Harvin describes her need to avoid conversations about race with her white friends and colleagues because she can no longer deal with their hurt, surprise, and defensiveness. Harvin relates an experience she had with a white woman in the public library who asked Harvin what she was working on. When Harvin explains that she is doing research on "raising black sons in this society,"[50] the white woman promptly inquires, "How is that any different from raising white sons?" As Harvin relates the encounter, she underscores that the white woman's question not only expressed a level of ignorance of the difficulties of raising a Black son in a white supremacist society but also that the tone, the skeptical manner, with which the question was framed implied in a condescending way that Harvin is "making something out of nothing."[51] Harvin chooses not to engage with the white woman and politely makes up an excuse that she is late and needs to leave the library—this was a conversation she could not have.

Hermeneutical injustice, Fricker's second type of epistemic injustice, occurs because "the powerful have an unfair advantage in structuring collective social understandings"[52] and this results in a lacuna (a gap) in the conceptual or linguistic resources of a society. According to Fricker, the absence of a concept to name an injustice results in marginally situated knowers not being able to understand or articulate what is happening to them because the language people use shapes how people make sense of their experiences. Significantly, Fricker attributes this lacuna to a structural identity prejudice in the collective hermeneutical framework.[53] If there is a lack of concepts in the collective hermeneutical resources to name injustice and the reason for this is structural identity prejudice, then marginally situated knowers do not have available to them the appropriate interpretative tools to understand and communicate their experiences. As an illustration of hermeneutical injustice, Fricker offers that before the term "sexual harassment" entered our public language, it was challenging for women to understand and name their experience of unwanted sexualized attention because their experience was rendered unintelligible due to gaps in the shared epistemic resources.

Although the lacuna exists for all knowers, according to Fricker, it does not manifest as injustice for dominantly situated knowers who find a fit between their experiences and the dominant resources available. Such lacunas when they exist, Fricker explains, are not the result of structural injustice that is based on the dominantly situated knower's social identity. It is interesting to note that Fricker equates "*collective* hermeneutical resources" or the shared concepts that are available to understand the social world with *dominant* hermeneutical frameworks, a point picked up by her critics.

An upsurge of scholarship exposing a lacuna in Fricker's own construal of hermeneutical injustice has deepened and enriched our understanding of this type of epistemic injustice. Because Fricker mistakenly associates dominant frameworks of intelligibility with the available *collective* hermeneutical resources, she fails to consider other frameworks of intelligibility that might be available to the marginally situated knower but not collectively recognized or even defiantly excluded by dominant frameworks. There is a *hidden* gap in Fricker's description of hermeneutical injustices because she assumes that if there are no epistemic resources in *dominant* frameworks of intelligibility (the collectively shared framework), then the marginally situated knowers will lack an understanding of their own experience.

As Rebecca Mason, Jose Medina, Gaile Pohlhaus Jr., and Kristie Dotson[54] have shown, marginally situated knowers often develop their own epistemic resources, concepts that make their experience intelligible among themselves. The real problem lies in that even when marginally situated knowers possess these concepts to name their experiences they may "still remain systematically misunderstood by others . . . when they try to communicate about those experiences."[55] This critique is significant because not only does it point to a limitation of Fricker's account, but it also shifts attention away from an exclusive focus on implicit identity bias and, instead, draws attention to *willful ignorance*, dominantly situated knowers' refusal to engage with resources that make sense of marginalized experience, as will subsequently be shown.

Since Fricker assumes only one collective hermeneutical framework, according to Dotson, she implies that both the marginally situated speaker and the dominantly situated hearer have equal difficulty in making marginalized experience intelligible.[56] Yet Dotson insists that this fails to recognize alternative epistemologies developed by marginalized communities that explain the injustices they experience but that are not widely accepted by dominantly situated knowers. More specifically, such alternative epistemologies are willfully resisted by dominantly situated knowers. Focusing on implicit bias alone as a source of epistemic injustice, as Fricker does, is another illustration of recentering dominantly situated knowers because, as will be emphasized in ensuing parts of this book, a focus on implicit bias protects dominantly situated knowers' comfort, innocence, and ignorance.

Pohlhaus significantly compliments Dotson's argument by explaining that dominantly situated knowers *pre-emptively* dismiss such epistemic resources and she introduces the concept of "willful hermeneutical ignorance" which occurs "when dominantly situated knowers refuse to acknowledge epistemic tools developed from the experienced world of those situated marginally."[57] This refusal to seriously engage allows dominantly situated knowers to "misunderstand, misinterpret, and/or ignore whole parts of the world."[58] The comfort of ignorance is, thus, preserved by such refusals.

Even when concepts that marginally situated knowers need to communicate their experience are in the collective understanding, they are often still misused or distorted. Pohlhaus offers that despite the existence of the term "sexual harassment" to name such oppression, some men will still dismiss the legitimacy of the term or mock women who use the term to explain their experience. Such men may dismiss women who use the term, blaming them for lacking a sense of humor or being too sensitive. They may even be described as "out on a witch hunt." In other words, even when the concepts are available to understand marginalized experience, they may not be adequately employed. These men protect their dominance by "not enter(ing) into a relation of true epistemic interdependence"[59] with the women who need this concept to explain their experience. While Fricker focuses on credibility deficit and contends that credibility excess does not constitute epistemic injustice, Pohlhaus demonstrates how dominantly situated knowers place *too much* confidence in their own experiences and interpretations of events and, thereby, cannot "hear" conflicting, but relevant, interpretations provided by marginally situated knowers.

Epistemic injustice thus involves more than just implicit bias or lack of concepts for marginally situated knowers to explain their experiences to themselves. Fricker's spotlight on implicit identity bias leads her to believe that if one just brings implicit bias to awareness, it will be distinguished. This ignores the resilience both of dominantly situated knowers' refusal to know as well as the closed character of dominant systems of meaning that contain the "seeds of their own preservation."[60] Dotson captures this when she introduces a third form of epistemic injustice that adds significantly to Fricker's testimonial and hermeneutical injustice. "Contributory injustice" underscores the *persistent deference* to dominant hermeneutical resources that prevents the proper uptake of the resources that the oppressed have developed to make sense of their experience.[61]

The emphasis on "contributory" highlights that this type of epistemic injustice is not about the marginally situated knower lacking adequate concepts to describe their experiences but rather that these concepts are *not taken up* by dominantly situated knowers and therefore do not effectively become part of collective understanding. The term "contributory" highlights at least two aspects of epistemic injustice. First, the emphasis put on "contributory" emphasizes to the state of affairs in which marginally situated knowers have a contribution to make to knowledge, but their contributions are systematically dismissed by dominantly situated knowers. Second, the term "contributory" underscores the ways in which the systemically privileged are *actively* and *collectively* complicit in blocking the conceptual resources from mainstream acceptance even when these resources are crucial for understanding marginalized experience. Attempts by marginally situated knowers to "prove" the pervasiveness of patterns of sexism and racism, for example, become tiresome and fruitless because there is no uptake or engagement. The rich scholarship on systemic white ignorance augments our understanding of how dominant conceptual and intellectual frameworks are maintained.

In his discussion of white ignorance, Charles Mills[62] argues that such ignorance is not merely a passive lack of knowledge on the part of the individual but a *structurally supported epistemology* that provides the individual with an entire battery of defense mechanism that supports an active distancing from what one does not want to know. Unlike traditional understandings of ignorance which consider ignorance as *individual* deficiency, Mills maintains that white ignorance is a form of *systemically* sustained ignorance that is "militant, aggressive, not at all confined to the illiterate and uneducated but propagating at the highest levels of the land, indeed presenting itself unblushingly as knowledge."[63] Linking white ignorance to the maintenance of white supremacy, Mills explains that dominant racial epistemic structures support "a particular pattern of localized and global cognitive dysfunctions (which are psychologically and socially functional) (that) protect the privileges of the racially dominant group and shield such privileges from contestation."[64]

Building and expanding upon Mills's work, Jose Medina[65] describes a type of active ignorance that clings to cognitive comfort and manifests in a refusal to believe that impedes learning and epistemic growth. Active ignorance protects comfortable certainties and "is a form of insensitivity that filters out experiences that can challenge out beliefs and create troubles for our cognitive perspective."[66] Active ignorance, Matt Whitt[67] expands and explains,

Functions less like a gap in knowledge or a conscious refusal to think, and more like a socially sanctioned and habituated way of being—a mode of actively, if unintentionally, . . . resisting new knowledge, counter-testimony, and recalcitrant experience.[68]

Active ignorance is often difficult to dislodge because it is concealed by meta-ignorance.

Medina introduces the concept of meta-ignorance to explain how bodies of ignorance remain resistant to change. Meta-ignorance involves an ignorance of one's own ignorance that ensures that dominantly situated knowers *will not have to* recognize how they are implicated in the perpetuation of unjust systems. This is an indication that dominant systems of meaning contain the seeds of their own preservation, as noted earlier. Mega-ignorance involves not only not knowing and not needing to know but, more significantly, *needing not to know*. For Medina, meta-ignorance entails an *active* effort to avoid what he refers to as "epistemic friction." Medina offers an analysis of "color-blindness" or the refusal to consider social positionality as an illustration of such avoidance of conflict and friction.

The point here is not that epistemic justice requires the uncritical acceptance of the testimony of marginally situated knowers (something that will be addressed in chapter 4) but, rather, to expose the ways in which dominantly situated knowers have the "privilege" to *immediately* doubt and dismiss the marginally situated speaker's testimony in ways that seem "reasonable." Meta-ignorance helps to bring an important feature of contributory injustice into clearer view because it not only reveals the self-confidence of individuals who do not know that they do not know and do not need to know marginalized truths but believe that they know, but it also highlights how dominantly situated knowers *need not to know* because to genuinely engage in such knowledge would threaten their epistemic comfort. Moreover, it underscores the *deeply built-in preserving mechanisms* that impede any attempt to challenge the authority of dominant frameworks of intelligibility.

The *willfulness* of willful ignorance now comes into sharper focus. Willfulness is not necessarily an *intentional* act of unwillingness, although it could be. Willful ignorance can be a tenacious refusal that does not seem like a refusal at all because it is buttressed by dominant epistemic frames. It is willful because it preserves epistemic comfort. In addition, it is an active form of ignorance that is not passive but actively reproduced by white people who believe that they know. Meta-ignorance as a form of willful ignorance is often maintained under the guise of objectivity, rationality, universality, and reasonableness. Appeals to rationality, Saba Fatima[69] underscores, "is often an attempt to reframe the incident to fit the worldview of the majority, such that the person making the appeal can remain blind to uncomfortable truths."[70]

The ways in which systemic injustice is justified by ostensibly "reasonable arguments" is a point accentuated in Dotson's recent article titled "Accumulating Epistemic Power: A Problem with Epistemology."[71] Dotson demonstrates how dominant concepts accumulate epistemic power that serve as the basis for "difficult-to-defeat arguments" reflecting a "resilient oblivion." These ways of arguing have the effect of normalizing oppressive conditions, in general, and in the case that Dotson critically analyzes, makes police slayings of Black people seem "reasonable."

To illustrate this point, Dotson breaks down the arguments publicly proffered by Joe Scarborough (a political commentator who is the co-host of the news show, *Morning Joe*) around the slaying of Michael Brown at the hands of Officer Darren Wilson. Scarborough argues that Brown is a "problematic victim" and supports his claim by pointing to "evidence" that any "reasonable" person would support. He argues that it follows that Officer Wilson's response that led to Brown's death was "legitimate" because Brown is not innocent. On this basis, Scarborough further maintains that the civil unrest that followed Brown's death was "unreasonable."

Dotson, however, establishes that Scarborough cherry-picks the evidence he is willing to consider, as he excludes from the category of "evidence" the larger structural context and systemic patterns in which Brown's death occurred. By doing so, Scarborough, and the epistemic power he wields, can remain oblivious to his complicity in the devaluing of Black lives. Why does it matter what Scarborough says, after all he is just one person? According to Dotson, the arguments of a person with systemic privilege and his public persona echo and reverberate in the minds of his followers, accumulating epistemic power along the way, as a snowball expands as it rolls down a snowy hill. Dotson's critical deconstruction of the rationalization of police brutality against Black bodies that hangs on the idea of "reasonable threat" offers a potent illustration of both willful ignorance and how patterns of oppressive events are recast as "reasonable" and, consequently, delegitimize and drown out alternative conceptual frameworks.[72]

Recently, Pohlhaus additionally considers the ways in which collective epistemic resistance to oppression is mistakenly reinterpreted as "behaving unreasonably or unthinkingly" and, thus, not deserving credibility. In "Gaslighting and Echoing, or Why Collective Epistemic Resistance is Not a 'Witch Hunt,'" Pohlhaus[73] offers a structural account of gaslighting and examines one type of such gaslighting which she refers to as epistemic gaslighting. Epistemic gaslighting occurs when a marginally situated knower's testimony is not afforded credibility so that a particular way of understanding the world, one that the testimony is an instance of, is put out of circulation.[74] Epistemic gaslighting is a form of epistemic injustice that reinforces meta-ignorance. The marginally situated knower gives testimony but then the listener's response is to question that testimony: "I know Jason, he would never do something like that" or "you must be overreacting." This is more than just dismissing marginalized testimony because the repetition of dismissal can lead the marginally situated knower to self-doubt, which is a fundamental aim of gaslighting. This resonates with the default skepticism that Nora Berenstain[75] emphasizes in her discussion of "epistemic exploitation."

Epistemic exploitation names the widespread experience (especially in academia) of systemically privileged individuals expecting marginally situated individuals to educate them about white privilege and the experience of oppression. Berenstain points to the ways in which such exploitation masquerades as epistemically virtuous forms of intellectual engagement—a pursuit of truth, a harmless exercise of curiosity, just wanting to know—but, in effect, such expectations are an abuse of marginalized people's labor. In addition, when the systemically privileged demand to be educated but then fail to utilize and seriously engage with what they are told, the epistemic harms of willful ignorance are not only intensified but dominant epistemic frameworks are also protected from challenges—all under the guise of the pursuit of knowledge.

Two related aspects of epistemic exploitation deserve emphasis. First, there is the unremunerated labor that marginally situated knowers are expected to provide to educate the systemically privileged about systems of privilege and oppression. This keeps marginally situated knowers busy with the needs and interests of privileged knowers while their own needs and academic interests are ignored. Second, in characterizing this labor, Berenstain draws attention not only to the labor of educating but also to the challenge that marginally situated knowers face in response to the testimony they offer. Berenstain refers to the "default skepticism of the privileged"[76] where the testimony of marginally situated knowers is not only responded to with suspicion but that, in the eyes of the skeptic, such skepticism is taken to be legitimate objections and even evidence of the skeptic being engaged and open-minded.

In light of these ostensibly good intentions, marginally situated knowers are forced into a dilemma—try harder to educate and endure the emotionally exhausting attempts to constantly justify and substantiate what one knows to those who do not have "the ears to hear" or be labeled negatively.[77] This echoes the argument made by Jones, previously discussed, about when marginally situated knowers refuse to educate, white students label *them* as the problem.[78] Dominantly situated knowers, in addition, do not only deny credibility to members of marginalized groups but they also demand information from marginally situated knowers which they then doubt in a way that keeps the rules of the game in dominantly situated knowers' hands.

These skeptical attitudes are a manifestation of willful ignorance and contribute to racial battle fatigue, the ubiquitous "physiological, psychological and behavioral strain exacted on racially marginalized and stigmatized groups and the amount of energy they expend coping with and fighting against racism."[79]

Saba Fatima describes an experience that concurs with how "reasonableness" can function to obscure what she is trying to say about racism. Fatima relates that one day as she worked as a teaching assistant, she ran into one of her students in the library who was studying for the final exam. The student was clearly anxious. In her attempt to calm her student's angst about the final, Fatima divulges to the student that she saw the exam and it's not that difficult. Another white male student standing nearby who was not in Fatima's section and overheard the conversation calls out to Fatima in a terse command, "Hey! . . . Come here." As a petite, woman of color and an advanced doctoral candidate the white male's student snippy tone felt jarringly disrespectful.

The point that Fatima underscores, however, is less about what the student did to her and more about the epistemic violence she encounters when she tries to explain to her colleagues why she felt so disrespected by the student's demand. Her interpretations of her experience are dismissed or reframed in ways that sound "reasonable" and, thus, difficult for her to counter. Fatima narrates that she is given advice such as "Be rational, be reasonable, the student didn't mean it that way" or "Don't make such a big deal out of something so trivial." Therefore, a common response of white people upon hearing about racially oppressive experiences is to offer alternate and "reasonable" explanation of what happened. The implication is that the speaker does not know how to describe his/her/their reality.[80]

Fatima explains how these *ostensibly well-meaning* and *seemingly reasonable* counsels push her to the edge of knowing and contribute to her questioning the reality she herself knows. Willful ignorance—a refusal to seriously engage with marginalized epistemic frameworks—plays a major part in the cycle that contributes to doubt and paranoia. Fatima notes that "we . . . become unsure . . . and lose epistemic ground with each passing moment because no one around us saw it the same way."[81] Given the epistemic costs, as previously noted, withdrawing from such hostile spaces is one way to enact a sense of agency and, also, is a form of self-survival.

In a similar way, white gaslighting or what some refer to as whitesplaining occurs when white people think they know better about marginalized experience than the marginalized. Gaslighting occurs when white people attempt to change the subject instead of engaging with a discussion of racism but sound like they are asking questions arising from genuine interest: "Don't you know that racism is over?" "But what about Black privilege?" "Why do you have this victim mindset?" "What about Black people who have made it—Densel, Obama, Oprah?" "If Black Lives Matter—what about Black on Black crime?" "Why are you always so angry?"

One additional way in which willful ignorance can be shielded from challenges through the tools of "reason" and "rationality" deserves mention. Recently, Ian Wekheiser[82] argues that *asking for reasons* can be weaponized as a mechanism of exclusion especially when criteria for justification are restricted by dominant frameworks. Drawing attention to what asking for reasons does in the context where the epistemically oppressed are not given uptake, Werkheiser offers an example of a conversation Audre Lorde and Adrienne Rich that highlights his point.

Audre: I've never forgotten the impatience in your voice that time on the telephone, when you said, "It's not enough to say to me that you intuit it." Do you remember? I will never forget that. Even at the same time that I understood what you meant, I felt a total wipeout of my modus, my way of perceiving and formulating.

Adrienne: Yes, but it's not a wipeout of your modus. Because I don't think my modus is unintuitive, right? And one of the crosses I've borne all my life is being told that I'm rational, logical, cool—I am not cool, and I'm not rational and logical in that icy sense. But there's a way in which, trying to translate from your experience to mine, I do need to hear chapter and verse from time to time. I'm afraid of it all slipping away into "Ah, yes, I understand you." . . .So if I ask for documentation, it's because I take seriously the spaces between us that difference has created, that racism has created. There are times when I simply cannot assume that I know what you know, unless you show me what you mean.

Audre: But I'm used to associating a request for documentation as a questioning of my perceptions, an attempt to devalue what I'm in the process of discovering.

Adrienne: It's not. Help me to perceive what you perceive. That's what I'm trying to say to you.

Audre: But documentation does not help one perceive. At best it only analyzes perception. At worst, it provides a screen by which to avoid concentrating on the core revelation, following it down to how it feels. Again, knowledge and understanding. They can function in concert, but they don't replace each other. But I'm not rejecting your need for documentation.[83]

Although Rich explains to Lorde that she often asks for "documentation" as a request to aid her understanding and not to deny Lorde's ideas, Lorde in return explains that requests for "documentation" feel to her like expressions of doubt because of the pattern of default skepticism that marginally situated knowers expect to encounter. Asking for reasons can be weaponized especially when criteria for justification are exclusively embedded in the dominant framework of intelligibility. Something that can seem as "reasonable" to dominantly situated knowers can simultaneously function to delegitimize alternative ways of knowing, whether dominantly situated knowers intentionally or unintentionally do so.

At this point, it should be clear that white individuals are less *subject to ignorance* and more coproducers of and agents in dominant frameworks of intelligibility, actively repressing and suppressing alternative ways of explaining the social world.[84] The white complicity claim is inherently connected to this active reproduction of ignorance and willful ignorance. The problem is the actively tenacious and exclusionary hold on white knowledge that reifies white ignorance. As Mills emphasizes, white ignorance is not a simple lack of knowledge that can be remedied with more knowledge but the active reproduction and protection of systemically dominant epistemological frameworks. Mills highlights that the invisible man in Ralph Ellison's book with that title is not invisible because he is a ghost. Rather, it is "simply because people *refuse* to see (him)."[85] This is an important point for the topic of my project. The question is how to negotiate this complicity without assuming it can be transcended and how to minimize or limit the harms that students of color endure because of such complicity.

Willful ignorance can be understood as the ultimate source of epistemic injustice. More than prejudice or implicit bias, it is dominant group members' denial of credibility to (and refusal to engage with) the frameworks of intelligibility that marginally situated knowers offer that supports epistemic injustice and shields such injustice from challenges, a point that Fricker's limited focus occludes. In the final section of this chapter, the relationship between protecting innocence and maintaining ignorance is elaborated to support the claim that ignorance cannot be disrupted so long as innocence is preserved.

INTERRUPTING INNOCENCE, UNSETTLING WILLFUL IGNORANCE

What can a white educator teaching about whiteness to white students learn from the scholarship on white innocence and white ignorance? Although discussed separately these two phenomena are related because the defense of white innocence makes it difficult for white people to critically interrogate white ignorance. In addition, the scholarship on active ignorance, meta-ignorance, and willful ignorance underscores how such ignorance is shielded from critique. The scholarship also makes clear that such ignorance serves to actively exclude serious engagement with concepts and ideas that marginally situated knowers have developed to explain their experience. For white students to be open to understanding what the racially marginalized say about their experiences with systemic white supremacy, they must first become less defensive about their innocence. When social justice educators help their white students to "lessen their innocence," as Fellows and Razack suggest, the prospect of learning about the systemic racial injustice that they help perpetuate becomes possible and opportunities to work in coalition with the racially marginalized to dismantle systemic white supremacy are created.

In his discussion of white distancing strategies, Matt Whitt argues that the source of white students' defensiveness is not only that they defend their innocence and deny their complicity. Whitt underscores that their defensiveness stems from a refusal to having their dominant world view that their lives are embedded in challenged. Distancing strategies, Whitt emphasizes, "Insulate students from having to consider that their world and their lives would be unrecognizable different without the very injustices they disavow."[86] Drawing on the work of Medina around active ignorance, described in this chapter, Whitt maintains that educators should focus on encouraging students to cultivate better epistemic habits.

Active ignorance, Whitt realizes is resilient to change. Active ignorance is a form of willful ignorance in which dominant frameworks of intelligibility authorize and support the resilience of ignorance. Dominant collective resources, as has been shown, have built-in defenses that are difficult to interrupt, and meta-ignorance makes ignorance seem like knowledge that masquerades as truth. Moreover, Whitt acknowledges that awareness-raising, while a valuable component of teaching, by itself will not disrupt active ignorance. As Whitt so aptly puts it, "Pedagogical approaches that focus on awareness-raising can backfire by giving students the impression of an epistemic conversion experience—they were once blind, but now they see."[87] Then, however, Whitt suggests that to ameliorate active ignorance "we need to meet students where they are. . . . I press their responses gently."[88] I will return to this suggestion in chapter 4 because white epistemic virtue must not come on the backs of students of color, a point that Whitt acknowledges and struggles with.[89]

The argument this chapter is making is that educators must first destabilize safeguards of white innocence so that their defensiveness toward alternative perspectives is decreased. If white innocence feeds into and serves as a fortification of willful ignorance, then innocence must be destabilized before white students can critically interrogate their role in maintaining ignorance. So long as white students cling to innocence, their defenses will block the ability to consider how the everyday practices of ordinary, good white people contribute to the perpetuation of institutions and structures that systemically benefit white people and, consequently, harm communities of color. In addition, without white students acknowledging how they are protective of their innocence, it will be difficult to form coalitions with people of color to fight for social change.

Disrupting innocence is crucial because even progressive white people who are working on being "antiracist" can reproduce whiteness. Even the acknowledgment of complicity can also function as a form of complicity. Drawing on J. L. Austin's theory of performative utterances in which an utterance performs an action in its being uttered, Sara Ahmed[90] argues that declarations of whiteness or public assertions of complicity are non-performatives. They do not accomplish the act that is spoken. In *publicly declaring* "I am racist" or "I am complicit," the white critic of whiteness confesses *something else*: "I am not racist" or "I am not complicit." Such confessions of white privilege or racism or complicity can take the place of action. All that is necessary is to confess. Nothing else needs to be done because the speech act establishes antiracist status. One's complicity in the oppressive everyday conditions of people of color can be ignored. In other words, the discursive effect of such non-performatives is that in confessing, it is as if one transcends the very thing confessed in the declaration.

Ahmed is not saying that in their declarations of whiteness, white people *do not mean* what they say. Instead, her point is that such assertions do not *do* what they say and do something else, something that presumes a "fantasy of transcendence." Ahmed cautions, "We need to consider the intimacy between privilege and the work we do, even in the work we do on privilege."[91] Therefore, Ahmed counsels, white individuals to be vigilant about how racial injustice can be reproduced even in the recognition of privilege as privilege, even when one thinks one is doing "good." Ahmed advises white students to "stay implicated in what they critique."[92]

The vigilance that is necessary for social justice education, and especially for teaching white students about their complicity in racism, therefore, must be a vigilance about *whites' own goodness*. The issue is more difficult than just increasing their critical thinking skills or epistemic virtues. In addition, because desires for white innocence block what white students can "hear," the development of diverse alliances with individuals and with groups for the purpose of collectively working toward racial change is impeded.

Ahmed makes concrete how desires for white innocence can obstruct what white people can hear. She points to a recurrent refrain from her white students, "But what should white people do?" At first sight, the asking of this question might seem like progress. As Ahmed explains,

> it can be an impulse to reconciliation as a "recovering" of the past (the desire to feel better); it can be about making public one's judgment ("what happened was wrong"); or it can be an expression of solidarity ("I am with you"); or it can simply be an orientation towards the openness of the future (rephrased as: "what can be done?").[93]

Yet the profound insight that Ahmed offers is that the question, "But what should white people do?" no matter how sincere or how well-intended can serve to allow the speaker to shift attention away from the critical issues being discussed and circumvent considering the ways in which the speaker is implicated in those issues. Ahmed continues to explain,

> But the question, in all of these modes of utterance, can work to block hearing; in moving on from the present towards the future, it can also move away from the object of critique, or place the white subject "outside" that critique in the present of the hearing. In other words, the desire to act, to move, or even to move on, can stop the message "getting through."[94]

White students will have a difficult time hearing what Ahmed is saying about their well-intended questions unless they have been introduced to what the rhetoric of white innocence does. If, paraphrasing Fiona Probyn,[95] acknowledging complicity is the starting point and the condition of the work whites need to do regarding social justice, then white people must first learn to be less protective about their innocence.

George Yancy narrates a pedagogical exercise he uses in his courses. He asks students to respond to the statement, "I am racist." Yancy is not asking his students to confess their racism but rather aiming to elicit students' meanings of racism and to prepare them for taking that question seriously. When most white students are quick to state that they are not racist, and they evidence that even applying that term to themselves is taboo, pondering this statement and, giving attention to whether and how it applies to oneself, makes possible a conversation that can begin to disrupt white innocence and, hopefully, result in a readiness to consider white complicity.

My claim that educators prioritize interrupting white innocence so that white students are primed to consider their complicity in systemic white supremacy does not imply aiming for "wokeness," the current pejorative term for consciousness-raising that alludes to a performative signaling of one's own self-interest. Pedagogies that primarily center awareness-raising are problematic. The individualist framework that grounds such approaches fails to contend with the deeper historical, cultural, and institutional dimensions of whiteness, something that will be addressed in more detail in the following chapter. Significantly, such approaches cannot help students to account for the enduring resilience of white practices and epistemic norms dominant in our society, or the way white power operates. In contrast, keeping the pedagogical focus on complicity ensures that the myriad ways white people are entangled with an unjust system, even and especially when they have good intentions, are at the forefront of pedagogy. It also assumes that there will be a strong focus on systemic white supremacy.

Recall Ahmed's exhortations that "declarations of whiteness" are "nonperformative." In other words, they do not do what the literal words intend them to do, challenge systemic privilege. Instead, they do something else—they preserve innocence. If white students are extraordinarily reluctant to perceive themselves in the position of oppressors, and if white innocence undeniably reverberates every time analyses of whiteness arise, then it follows that the initial pedagogical objective should be to help white students realize that the effects of their good intentions may not be transparent to them. This is crucial to consider because these effects are experienced as violence to students of color. Yet, as we shall discuss in chapter 4, addressing white educational needs risks recentering whiteness.

Disrupting innocence allows white students to consider their complicity within oppressive systems and how they contribute to the harm of racial injustice. This call to develop a deep understanding of the ways in which white peoples' good intentions are positioned within oppressive structures increases the prospect of working in coalitions toward undoing these structures.

In his critique of antiracist education that focuses on white privilege, Zeus Leonardo[96] insists that the starting point for teaching white students should be white supremacy and white domination rather than white privilege. White supremacy, according to Leonardo involves the "direct processes that secure domination and the privileges associated with it."[97] I read this to mean that white students' learning must begin with an acknowledgment of white complicity rather than white privilege. According to Leonardo, white supremacy is the condition that makes systemic privilege possible. By existing and benefiting from white supremacy, white people are complicit in a system that oppresses people of color. Complicity entails connections between the personal and the structural, the individual and the collective.

Leonardo maintains that white students' learning must begin with an acknowledgment of white people as active oppressors and perpetuators of unjust systems rather than a focus on unearned privileges. A focus on white privilege, Leonardo argues, implies passivity buttressed by the notion of *unearned* white advantages. When white privilege is described as a knapsack or as similar "to walking down the street with money being put into your pant pocket without your knowledge,"[98] it conveys the message that white people are passive and unknowing. This transfers the attention away from the oppression of the racially marginalized and obscures the complicity of white people in that oppression. Subsequently, if the emphasis is on passively receiving privilege, the ways in which white people are currently, and perpetually, active agents in the maintenance of white supremacy/white dominance can be concealed.

While Leonardo recognizes that the advantage of white privilege discourse is that it encourages whites to be more receptive and it limits white guilt (he assigns McIntosh's article in his courses, but then critiques it with his students), he nevertheless argues that a concentration on privilege hides the ways in which whites play an active role in the domination of people of color. When the discourse surrounding white privilege is constructed in such a way as to remove white responsibility and complicity in the maintenance of white power, the subject of domination as an agent of actions is obscured.

Courtenay Daum[99] also emphasizes white complicity. She argues that demands for institutional change require individual and sociocultural change. Daum insists that focusing on disrupting white innocence and encouraging the acknowledgment of white complicity need not necessarily divert attention away from systemic racial injustice. Rather, Daum emphasizes that if white people are not willing to critically problematize their investments in maintaining the system, then they will continue to reproduce the system of racial injustice and continue to deny the lived reality of people of color's experiences.

It is important to emphasize that acknowledging white complicity is futile without a willingness to contribute to concrete systematic change and commitments to political action. Consciousness-raising can result in nothing more than navel-gazing aiming at personal introspection rather than a way of transforming systemic racial injustice. Self-reflection is ultimately less demanding than contributing to durable political coalitions and it may even be therapeutic. In addition, as Ahmed and others insist, antiracist education must begin with the works of scholars of color who make it abundantly clear how whiteness is experienced by the racially marginalized.

This section begins to explore what the scholarship around white innocence and white ignorance can offer white educators who teach white students about whiteness. Ahmed's exhortation is significant because even when white educators acknowledge that they are complicit in racial injustice, even if unwittingly, it does not mean that white educators transcend their complicity. The question of how to stay implicated in what they critique becomes crucial. What insights can this body of scholarship offer to the white educators teaching students of color?

GOOD WHITE INTENTIONS MATTER, BUT THEIR EFFECTS MATTER MORE

This chapter made explicit the link between preserving white innocence and the perpetuation of white willful ignorance and highlighted the problem of good white intentions mattering more than their effects. It is not that white people should not have good intentions but rather that good white intentions must be understood against the background of systematic power hierarchies that precede those intentions and affect their effects. Clinging to the goodness of these intentions can obscure one's continuing participation in systems of racial domination not only in those who display empty commitments to racial justice but also in those who earnestly want to do better.

White complicity envelops white educators who teach and interrogate whiteness with a racially diverse body of students. In chapter 4, some of the challenging pedagogical questions that arise that follow from this claim will be addressed. For now, the scholarship on white innocence and white ignorance alerts the white educator teaching about whiteness that good white intentions can conceal the harmful effects of those intentions on students of color. When white educators and white students are focused on their good intentions, it can be difficult to seriously engage with what students of color are trying to communicate not only about their experiences with systemic white supremacy in society at large but also, in the classroom, more specifically. It is not that good intentions do not matter, but rather recognizing that good intentions do not transcend the social context in which they are embedded and, thus as Ahmed makes clear, they may block what one is willing to understand.

While the scholarship does not seem to offer much regarding recommendations about how to lessen white innocence, there are many references to cultivating humility in the scholarship. Moreover, numerous recommendations for how to remedy epistemic injustice have been offered. In the next chapter, attention is turned to recommendations offered to alleviate epistemic injustice and white ignorance. In chapter 4, what insights the white educator can glean from these recommendations will be discussed and what kind of challenges that may arise for the white educator from those recommendations will be addressed.

NOTES

1. George Yancy, "Dear White America." *The New York Times* (December 24, 2015).

2. Terese Jonsson, *Innocent Subjects: Feminism and Whiteness* (Pluto Press, 2021).

3. Thomas Ross, "The Rhetorical Tapestry of Race: White Innocence and Black Abstraction." *William & Mary Law Review* 32, no. 1 (1990): 1–40.

4. Ibid., 3

5. As cited in Ross, ibid., 9.

6. Ibid., 498. Hunt quoting Seth Harris, "Innocence and the Sopranos." *New York Law School Law Review* 49 (2005): 577 who is quoting from *The Oxford English Dictionary* (2nd edition, 1989): 995.

7. Cecil J. Hunt II, "The Color of Perspective: Affirmative Action and the Constitutional Rhetoric of White Innocence." *Michigan Journal of Race and Law* 11 (2006): 477–555.

8. Ruth Frankenberg, *White Women, Race Matters: The Social Construction of Whiteness* (Minneapolis, MN: University of Minnesota Press, 1993). Frankenberg uses this term to describe white women who insist on emphasizing sameness among women and ignore the differences race make to one's lived experiences.

9. Richard Orozco and Jesus Jaime Diaz, "'Suited to their Needs': White Innocence as a Vestige of Segregation." *Multicultural Perspectives* 18, no. 3 (2016): 127–133.

10. Gloria Wekker, *White Innocence: Paradoxes of Colonialism and Race* (London: Duke University Press, 2017).

11. Ibid., 2.

12. Mary Louise Fellows and Sherene Razack, "The Race to Innocence: Confronting Hierarchical Relations Among Women." *Journal of Gender, Race and Justice*, 1 (1998): 335–352.

13. Ibid., 335.

14. Ibid., 152.

15. Sarita Srivastava, "'You're Calling Me a Racist?' The Moral and Emotional Regulation of Anti-Racism and Feminism." *Signs: Journal of Women and Culture in Society* 31, no. 1 (2005): 29–62.

16. Ibid., 31.

17. Sara Ahmed, *On Being Included: Racism and Diversity in Institutional Life* (Durham: Duke University Press, 2012).

18. Ibid., 1.

19. Ibid., 14.

20. Ibid., 41.

21. Ibid., 147.

22. Sara Ahmed, *The Promise of Happiness* (Durham: Duke University Press, 2010).

23. Ibid., 65.

24. Sara Ahmed, *On Being Included*, 49.

25. Sara Ahmed, *The Promise of Happiness*, 68.

26. Ibid.

27. Sara Ahmed, "Rocking the Boat: Women of Colour as Diversity Workers." In Jason Arday and Heidi Safia Mirza, eds., *Dismantling Race in Higher Education: Racism, Whiteness and Decolonsing the Academy* (New York: Palgrave, 2018): 331–348.

28. Ibid., 339.

29. Ruby Hamad, *White Tears/Brown Scars: How White Feminism Betrays Women of Color* (New York: Catapult, 2020).

30. Audre Lorde, *Sister Outsider* (Freedom, CA: Crossing Press, 1984): 125.

31. Alison Jones, "The Limits of Cross-Cultural Dialogue: Pedagogy, Desire, and Absolution in the Classroom." *Educational Theory* 49, no. 3 (1999): 299–316.

32. Ibid., 312.

33. Ibid.
34. Ibid., 302.
35. Maria Lugones and Elizabeth Spelman, "Have We Got a Theory for You! Feminist Theory, Cultural Imperialism and the Demand for 'the Woman's Voice.'" *Women's Studies International Forum* 6, no. 6 (1983): 573–581.
36. Ibid., 576.
37. Leslie Roman, "Denying (White) Racial Privilege: Redemption Discourses and the Use of Fantasy." In M. Fine (ed.), *Off White: Readings on Race, Power and Society* (New York: Routledge, 1997): 270–282.
38. Charles Mills, *The Racial Contract* (Ithaca, NY: Cornell University Press, 1997).
39. Deanna Blackwell, "Sidelines and Separate Spaces: Making Education Anti-Racist for Students of Color," *Race, Ethnicity, and Education* 13, no. 4 (2010): 473–494.
40. Miranda Fricker, *Epistemic Injustice: Power and the Ethics of Knowing* (Oxford: Oxford University Press, 2007).
41. Miranda Fricker, "Epistemic Justice as a Condition of Political Freedom." *Synthese* 190 (2013): 1317–1332.
42. Lorraine Code, *Rhetorical Spaces: Essays on Gendered Locations* (London: Routledge, 1995); Patricia Hill Collins, *Black Feminist Thought: Knowledge, Consciousness, and the Politics of Empowerment* (London: Routledge, 1990); Linda Alcoff and Elizabeth Potter, eds., *Feminist Epistemologies* (New York: Routledge. 1993).
43. Fricker, *Epistemic Injustice*, 1.
44. Ibid., 158.
45. Harper Lee, *To Kill a Mockingbird* (Philadelphia, PA; Lippincott, 1960).
46. Gaile Pohlhaus Jr., "Discerning the Primary Epistemic Harm in Cases of Testimonial Injustice," *Social Epistemology* 28, no. 2 (2014): 99–114.
47. Kristie Dotson, "Tracking Epistemic Violence, Tracking Practices of Silencing." *Hypatia* 26, no. 2 (2011): 236–257.
48. Reni Eddo-Lodge, *Why I'm No Longer Talking to White People About Race* (New York: Bloomsbury, 2017).
49. Cassandra Byers Harvin, "Conversations I Can't Have" *On the Issues* 5, no. 2 (1996): 15–16.
50. Ibid., 16.
51. Ibid.
52. Fricker, *Epistemic Injustice*, 147.
53. Fricker, 155.
54. Jose Medina, "Hermeneutical Injustice and Polyphonic Contextualism: Social Silences and Shared Hermeneutical Responsibilities." *Social Epistemology* 26, no. 2 (2012): 201–220; Gaile Pohlhaus Jr. "Relational Knowing and Epistemic Injustice: Toward a Theory of Willful Hermeneutical Ignorance." *Hypatia* 27, no. 4 (2012): 715–735; Kristie Dotson, "A Cautionary Tale: On Limiting Epistemic Oppression." *Frontiers: A Journal of Women Studies* 33, no. 1 (2012): 24–47; Rebecca Mason, "Two Kinds of Unknowing." *Hypatia* 26, no. /2 (2011): 294–307. It should be

noted that in more recent work, Fricker has acknowledged the significance of both Pohlhaus's and Dotson's critique. See Miranda Fricker, "Evolving Concepts of Epistemic Injustice." In J. Kidd, J. Medina, and G. Pohlhaus, eds., *The Routledge Handbook of Epistemic Injustice* (New York: Routledge, 2017): 53–60.

55. Jose Medina. "Hermeneutical Injustice and Polyphonic Contextualism," 207.
56. Kristie Dotson, "A Cautionary Tale."
57. Gaile Pohlhaus Jr., "Relational Knowing and Epistemic Injustice," 715.
58. Ibid., 716.
59. Ibid., 726.
60. Alison Bailey, "The Unlevel Knowing Field: An Engagement with Dotson's Third-Order Epistemic Oppression." *Social Epistemology Review and Reply Collective* 3, no. 10 (2014): 62–68, 66.
61. Dotson, "A Cautionary Tale."
62. Charles Mills, "White Ignorance," In Shannon Sullivan and Nancy Tuana, eds., *Race and Epistemologies of Ignorance* (Albany, NY: State University of New York Press, 2007): 13–38.
63. Ibid., 13.
64. Ibid., 18.
65. Jose Medina, *The Epistemology of Resistance: Gender and Racial Oppression, Epistemic Injustice, and Resistant Imaginations* (New York: Oxford University Press, 2013); Jose Medina, "On Refusing to Believe: Insensitivity and Self-Ignorance." In José María Ariso and Astrid Wagner, eds., *Rationality Reconsidered: Ortega y Gasset and Wittgenstein on Knowledge, Belief, and Practice* (Berlin: De Gruyter, 2016): 187–200.
66. Medina, "On Refusing to Believe," 192.
67. Matt Whitt, "Other People's Problems: Student Distancing, Epistemic Responsibility, and Injustice." *Studies in Philosophy and Education* 35, no. 5 (2016): 427–444.
68. Ibid., 432.
69. Saba Fatima, "On the Edge of Knowing: Microaggressions and Epistemic Uncertainty as a Woman of Color." In Kirsti Cole and Holly Hassel, eds., *Surviving Sexism in Academia: Feminist Strategies for Leadership* (New York: Routledge 2017): 147–154.
70. Ibid., 149.
71. Kristie Dotson, "Accumulating Epistemic Power: A Problem with Epistemology." *Philosophical Topics* 46, no .1 (2018): 129–154.
72. One need only watch the trial of former police officer Derek Chauvin charged with the murder of George Floyd in Minneapolis, Minnesota, on May 25, 2020, to understand that Dotson's argument exposes a pattern of attempts to justify and cover up systemic racial injustice through ostensibly "reasonable" arguments.
73. Gaile Pohlhaus Jr., "Gaslighting and Echoing, or Why Collective Epistemic Resistance is not a 'Witch Hunt.'" *Hypatia* 35, no. 4 (2020): 674–686.
74. Ibid., 677.
75. Nora Berenstain, "Epistemic Exploitation." *Ergo* 3, no. 22 (2016): 569–590.
76. Berenstain, 578.

77. Alison Jones, "The Limits of Cross-Cultural Dialogue." 308.
78. Ibid.
79. William A. Smith, "Higher Education: Racial Battle Fatigue." In R. T. Schaefer, ed., *Encyclopedia of Race, Ethnicity, and Society* (Thousand Oaks, CA: Sage, 2008): 615–618, 617.
80. Fatima, "On the Edge of Knowing," 152.
81. Ibid., 148.
82. Ian Wekheiser, "Asking for Reasons as a Weapon: Epistemic Justification and the Loss of Knowledge." *Journal of Cognition and Neuroethics* 2, no. 1 (2014): 173–190.
83. Audre Lorde, *Sister Outsider* (New York: Ten Speed Press, 1984): 103–102 as cited by Wekheiser, ibid., 188–189.
84. Zeus Leonardo, "The Myth of White Ignorance." In his *Race, Whiteness and Education* (New York: Routledge, 2009): 107–125.
85. Ralph Waldo Ellison, *Invisible Man* (New York: Vintage, 1995): 3.
86. Matt Whitt, "Other People's Problems," 428.
87. Ibid., 437.
88. Ibid., 438.
89. Ibid. 440.
90. Sara Ahmed, "Declarations of Whiteness: The Non-Performativity of Anti-Racism," *Borderlands e-journal* 3, no. 2 (2004), http://www.borderlandsejournal.adelaide.edu.au/vol3no2_2004/ahmed_declarations.htm
91. Ibid.
92. Sara Ahmed, "Declarations of Whiteness."
93. Ibid.
94. Ibid.
95. Fiona Probyn, "Playing Chicken at the Intersection: The White Critic in/of Critical Whiteness Studies," *Borderlands* 13, no. 2 (2004). http://www.borderlandse-journal.adelaide.edu.au/vol3no2_2004/probyn_playing.htm (accessed July 19, 2009).
96. Zeus Leonardo, "The Colour of Supremacy: Beyond the Discourse of 'White privilege.'" *Educational Philosophy and Theory* 36, no. 2 (2004): 137–152.
97. Ibid., 137.
98. Leonardo relates how James Scheurich, an anti-racist educational researcher, described whiteness in this way. Ibid., 138.
99. Courtenaqy W. Daum, "White Complicity." *New Political Science* 42, no. 3 (2020): 443–449.

Chapter 3

Toward a Vigilantly Vulnerable Informed Humility

"Killing White Innocence" is the title of Stephen Brookfield's[1] review of George Yancy's book *Backlash: What Happens When We Talk Honest About Racism*. Brookfield begins the review by relating a story about a white friend, a woman who spent forty years engaged in literary education in both Harlem and Washington Heights in New York City and was a tireless advocate of the people of color she worked with. This white woman tells Brookfield about an antiracist workshop she recently attended where she was required to stand up and say, "I am racist." Although Sara Ahmed's work points to the dangers of such an exercise (as discussed in the previous chapter), Brookfield's point in narrating this story is focused not on the exercise but on his white friend's response. Brookfield notes that his friend recounted this event in anger, and as he puts it, "She couldn't believe that her four decades of anti-racist endeavors had been discounted by these facilitator-strangers who didn't know anything about her." She refused to remain in the workshop and left immediately.

For Brookfield, a white educational theorist whose work in antiracist education is well-known, this story has resonances with some aspects of the backlash accentuated in the title of Yancy's book. Yancy wrote a letter in the *New York Times* calling on white people to acknowledge the ways they are implicated in benefiting from and upholding "a complex web of racist power relationships . . . heteronomous webs of white practices to which you, as white, are linked both as beneficiary and as co-contributor to such practices."[2] The vicious backlash Yancy underwent because of this letter serves as a reflection of the ways that white people are unwilling to consider their active investment in maintaining systemic racial injustice all the while actively perpetuating such injustice. In Brookfield's story, his friend, who considers herself an ally to people of color, cannot fathom that she can also be perpetrating practices that reproduce racial injustice, even when her white denial is a manifestation of such reproduction.

At least two dangers surface when white people conceive themselves as allies to people of color. First, as Brookfield intimates, being an ally is a designation that is "not ever ours to make."[3] To be an ally is not determined by white people but by the ones whom one is trying to be an ally to. It is not only arrogant for white people to claim their own allyship but also a reiteration of white power and privilege. As Christopher Bridges and Peter Mather contend, "The ability to call oneself ally rests on privilege."[4] Second, and related to the first, Brookfield explains that focusing on one's good intentions is a recentering of the white self. Brookfield notes how he tells himself that "I should not get so hung up on how I'm feeling because, after all, it's not really about me, is it?" Brookfield recommends that white individuals cultivate humility to facilitate the lessening of white recentering that protects white innocence.

In this chapter, cultivating humility as a tool for disrupting white innocence and for unsettling white ignorance is examined. Traditional analyses of humility allude to two features of humility: avoiding arrogance by not recentering one's own needs/interests and owning one's limitations. Both these aspects are analyzed in a very individualistic way in the traditional philosophical scholarship and these studies do not take social position into consideration. The point of not recentering one's own needs/interests *merge with* owning one's limitations when the worry is about the harms of dominant frameworks of intelligibility that allow dominant knowers to not know but think they know, to not need to know, and, as previously discussed, to need not to know how they are implicated in systemic injustice.

Moreover, the call for humility in the context of whiteness is not an untethered relativism where all epistemic frameworks must be given voice. The humility advocated for unsettling systemic white supremacy and the acknowledgment of one's limitations does not entail that all viewpoints are equally valid. Instead, the call for humility is about cultivating an attitude of openness to alternative views that are systematically excluded by dominant epistemologies. Alison Bailey exposes the individualistic character of such conceptions of humility and suggests a type of humility that is grounded in vulnerability. Bailey's exploration of humility is discussed and her emphasis on the relational dimension of humility is detailed.

The dangers of individualistic approach to social and epistemic injustice are further drawn out by critically examining Miranda Fricker's remedy for epistemic injustice, that is, developing a sensitivity that entails an awareness of bias and being able to correct for it. Fricker's focus on identity prejudice or implicit bias is shown to be limited and insidious because its focus on identity bias obscures the ways in which systemic conditions enable such bias. Furthermore, the focus on identity prejudice ignores how willful ignorance on the part of dominant knowers contributes to epistemic injustice. Just like the problems with implicit bias training (IBT), Fricker's recommendations for sensitivity risk leading to confessions that reproduce injustice instead of disrupting it.

Remedies for epistemic injustice that do not take seriously, systemically sanctioned ignorance are problematic. Therefore, the discussion turns to an examination of Jose Medina's suggested remedies for epistemic injustice which take active and meta-ignorance seriously. Medina's recommendations and the virtues he advances, however, are critically assessed. Some concerns are raised about his emphasis on epistemic friction. Since one of the virtues that Medina recommends is open-mindedness, some of the scholarships around that topic is discussed. The recent work on open-mindedness, we find, returns us to the concept of vulnerability.

In the final section, a vigilantly vulnerable informed humility is introduced as a means of combating white innocence and white ignorance. Developing this type of humility can help dominantly situated knowers navigate staying in and learning from the acknowledgment of complicity and can be a counter to willful ignorance and defensive innocence. In chapter 4, how white educators negotiate complicity and some of the challenges they encounter when teaching about whiteness to racially diverse students are examined. The aim of chapter 4 is to apply the insights of the previous chapters to the pedagogical cases that white educators indicate are challenging for them.

HUMILITY MUST NOT RECENTER WHITENESS

In the past, philosophers have shown intermittent interest in the meaning and significance of humility as a virtue.[5] As far back as the early Greek philosophers, Socrates was famously known for his abhorrence of intellectual arrogance and he is commonly known for claiming that the only true wisdom is in knowing you know nothing. Recently, there has been an upsurge of interest in the virtue of humility and an edited volume on the philosophy of humility has been published reflecting this renewed interest.[6] A focus on the relationship between the concepts of humility and modesty has sharpened the definition of humility.[7] Philosophers have debated whether humility requires having a low opinion of oneself and an underestimation of one's self-worth or whether humility is just about generally being less self-centered.[8] There has also been extended attention to what Brian Robinson[9] refers to as the "paradox of humility," that is, that professing humility, even correctly, is proof that one is not humble. Feminist scholars have even debated whether humility can be a liberatory virtue.[10]

As Brookfield suggests in the story that opens this chapter, cultivating humility is thought to be corrective to a form of arrogance in which white people, especially those with antiracist credentials, deny their complicity in systemic racism. Humility, however, risks recentering whiteness even when the humble person has good intentions. In her discussion of white feminists who consider themselves inclusive and anti-oppression but essentialize being a woman as if all women were white, Elizabeth Spelman describes what she refers to as boomerang perspective or the practice of "I look at you and come right back to myself."[11] Cultivating humility, thus, requires foregrounding the need to decenter the self. One way suggested to decenter the self has been to own one's limitations.

In the philosophical scholarship, the characteristic feature of humility has been owning one's limitations. Daniel Whitcomb, Heather Battaly, Jason Baehr, and Daniel Howard-Snyder,[12] specifically focused on intellectual humility, offer that humility involves "having the right stance towards one's limitation."[13] While the question of the limits of humility is often debated, Whitcomb et al. insist that humility understood as a virtue entails taking responsibility for one's own limitations for the right reason, at the right time, and in the right way.

These two attributes associated with humility, that is, a decentering of the self/ego, and an acknowledgment of one's epistemic limits, are related in that an arrogance and self-centeredness can lead to a failure to acknowledge one's limits. While helpful, these understandings of humility assume a decontextualized subject who can develop humility in isolation of others. Moreover, a lack of humility or being arrogant is often primarily attributed to personal deficiency without consideration of the social structures within which these traits develop.

In the context of systemic white supremacy, the concern is not only with the limitations of one's own intellectual abilities but also one's connection to dominant epistemic frameworks whose strict boundaries discount and reject alternate epistemic frameworks, and mystifies this so it does not seem as this is what is happening. John Greco[14] hints at this when he argues that the individualistic approach to humility presumes humility is entirely a function of what is in the individual's mind. Instead, Greco contends that humility is "a function of her own mind, together with how that mind is causally and otherwise related to the world."[15] In his critique of epistemic individualism and epistemic internalism that embraces the ideal of intellectual self-sufficiency, Greco argues that humility is an appreciation of own intellectual ability plus the acceptance of our epistemic dependence on others. Greco's argument intimates that epistemic arrogance can be a function of dominant structures of knowledge but does not go far enough. Recall that Jose Medina argues that those who are embedded in meta-ignorance erroneously believe that they know and, in this sense, demonstrate epistemic arrogance.

Eschewing a predominantly individualistic conception of humility, Alison Bailey[16] draws out the relational dimension of this esteemed virtue and links humility to the recent scholarship on vulnerability. By doing so she puts systems of power and positionality at the foreground of her analysis. Bailey is replying to a provocative essay by Samantha Vice titled "How Do I Live in This Strange Place,"[17] describing Vice, a white South African woman, as a scholar who recognizes that without understanding her white complicity in systemic racial injustice, good white actions "risk falling back into unreflective do-gooding, rescuing, controlling, fixing, and missionary responses that allow us to restore our goodness (at least in our own minds)."[18]

Bailey relates that one of the strategies that Vice advocates to minimize these risks is cultivating humility. According to Bailey, however, for humility to avoid the dangers of restoring moral goodness or white solipsism, the interdependent or relational understandings of the white subject and white practices must be acknowledged. Borrowing a quote from Barbara Houston, Bailey cautions whites like Vice who struggle with what responsibility for complicity requires, "Do not take responsibility unaccompanied by those who can show you your part in the harm."[19]

The relational dimension of humility is key for white individuals who want to better understand the harmful effects of their good intentions. Bailey insists that white people need "disagreeable mirrors"[20] (recall Yancy's similar insistence in his letter to white people) often available if one takes seriously what people of color say and what they write about their experiences with systemic racism. Such mirrors can encourage white people to better understand the effects of their intentions and, in this case, the effects of their enactment of humility.

Bailey puts a strong focus on recognizing the effects of our practices and interactions rather than recentering the self. She explains:

> My point is not to reduce people of color to the function of reliable mirrors for the purposes of white consciousness-raising; that would be a non-relational account. The shift is not from "what do I think about me" to "what do *you* think about me." It is about our interactions and what they reveal about race.[21]

Bailey alludes to the dangers of humility recentering whiteness. One suggestion that Bailey offers to deflect such recentering is to recognize that people have multiple selves. White individuals often resist considering some aspects of their selves that the experiences of people of color compel white people to confront. Bailey attempts to develop a form of humility that can thwart such resistance by linking humility to a type of vulnerability advanced by Erinn Gilson.[22]

According to Gilson, vulnerability is not something negative and to be avoided but, instead, a quality of being open to seeing and being seen in ways and that such humility as vulnerability can challenge white self-conceptions. Gilson contends that vulnerability is not only about weakness, defenselessness, and being susceptible to injury but also about openness to others. For Bailey, humility, as grounded in vulnerability, is "always an openness before someone." The idea of "being open to others" is also prominent in calls for open-mindedness. Gilson's notion of vulnerability is relevant for understanding humility as open-mindedness and her work will be taken up again in the section addressing open-mindedness.

Bailey's emphasis on the relational dimension of humility and the significance of vulnerability underscores two substantial points. First, it makes clear that combating systemic white supremacy through virtues that are *primarily* about inner-directed work and consciousness-raising risks recentering white feelings. Her insistence on the relational dimension of humility exposes that primarily focusing on the individual can obstruct the need to reflect upon the connection between individuals, on the one hand, and the social context and power systems within which they are embedded in or constituted, on the other. Second, humility as being open to "disagreeable mirrors" highlights that the type of uncertainty that humility might call for is an openness that questions a particular type of certainty that is related to dominant structures. Her call for humility informed by vulnerability is a humility that avoids closure so that considering one's position in social structures and the effects of one's positionality become possible.

This discussion of vulnerable humility offers a segue to the complex discussion of the role of epistemic tension and a vigilant willingness to stay in uncomfortable moments to effectively learn about how deeply whites are infected by whiteness, a point that is also taken up by Jose Medina in his discussion of white ignorance. First, however, a brief detour to examine Miranda Fricker's[23] remedies for testimonial injustice will serve as the background for the constructive insights that Medina offers and corroborates the problem of taking a primarily individualistic approach to remedying white innocence and white ignorance.

REMEDIATING IMPLICIT BIAS IS NOT ENOUGH

Identity prejudice, according to Fricker, plagues epistemic injustice, in general, and, more specifically, testimonial injustice. As a remedy for identity prejudice, Fricker advances testimonial sensibility, a type of corrective testimonial justice that has two components. First, the receiver of testimony is required to reflect upon and be critically aware of when identity prejudice is impacting credibility judgments. As Fricker notes, when the "hearer suspects prejudice in her credibility judgment . . . she should shift intellectual gear out of spontaneous, unreflective mode and into active critical reflection in order to identify how far the suspected prejudice has influenced her judgment."[24] Second, the receiver of testimony must correct for this bias, "to reliably neutralize prejudice in her judgments of credibility."[25] Fricker recommends that the hearer compensate "upwards" until the appropriate credibility they would give to the speaker if it were not for the bias of the stereotype that is influencing the judgment is reached. The individual is assumed to be able to recognize identity prejudice, and especially when it is pointed out, and to adjust credibility upwards to the appropriate level of credibility judgment. Fricker explains that in cases where we cannot readjust our biased judgments that the best course of action is to "suspend judgment altogether or seek more evidence."[26]

Fricker is focused on a specific type of bias that "tend(s) surreptitiously to inflate or deflate the credibility afforded the speaker" and pertains to "social identity."[27] In contemporary terms, the type of prejudice that Fricker points to is often referred to as implicit bias. Implicit bias is understood as pre-conscious associations that affect how individuals can act in a way that produce discriminatory and inequitable outcomes for different identity groups and their members. Since implicit bias is unconscious and can have an impact on judgment and action, even well-intentioned individuals can unknowingly act in ways that reflect implicit, rather than explicit, bias.[28] The remedy Fricker proposes correlates with the remedy that is proposed by those who address correcting implicit bias. There are various concerns with a view that focuses on personal prejudice or bias, prominent among these is that any prescription for alleviating epistemic injustice that is excessively individualistic results in an under-appreciation of the structural dimensions of epistemic oppression.[29]

Rae Langton[30] offers a powerful and pertinent critique of Fricker's remedies for epistemic injustice. Langton contends that Fricker's excessive focus on individual remedies downplays consideration of the structural dimensions of oppression. Fricker, according to Langton, "offers us an *individual* remedy—epistemic virtue—in response to individual and structural vices."[31] Identity prejudice, a form of implicit bias, is a product of structural features and, not only, individual ones. While exposing identity prejudice and cultivating a disposition to be critically aware of when our judgments are influenced by them is important, so long as structural dimensions of epistemic injustice remain unchallenged, Langton maintains, real epistemic justice will not be achieved.

Langton's point is especially pertinent today when a prominent trend in higher education and in other corporate venues is to focus on implicit bias as an antidote for toxic campus and corporate climates. Fricker, like many of those in higher education and the corporate world, reduces patterns of injustice to bias in the individual speaker's mind. In chapter 1, it has been noted that definitions of racism that are primarily focused on prejudice are inadequate because such definitions obscure the structures within which those biases are embedded. Although Fricker takes social identity into consideration, her view under-explores how the one who receives testimony as well as the one who gives testimony are situated in and constituted by larger structures of power, privilege, and oppression. Most significantly, her focus on identity prejudice overlooks the influence of willful ignorance, as described in the previous chapter.

We can observe similar drawbacks in the IBT that is often the go-to-cure to improve hostile environments. A critical component of such training is the identification of unconscious prejudices in the minds of individuals that impact behavior. A central feature of training programs that primarily focus on implicit bias involves unknowing. Making what is unknown visible to the one who is unaware of the bias that influences behavior is the goal of IBT. Although IBT can compel individuals to become aware of biases that they do not know that they hold, a danger of IBT, ironically, is that systemic ignorance can be protected rather than disrupted and corrected. Several scholars[32] have called for a shift in focus from *lack of knowledge* to a *willful resistance to know*.

Lacey Davidson[33] argues that approaches such as Fricker that are primarily concerned with implicit bias without considering the larger social context risk assuming that IBT alone can be the remedy for social injustice. Using Kristie Dotson's[34] terminology, Davidson explains that there are three levels of epistemic exclusion that result in epistemic oppression and injustice. First-order exclusions result when the dominant epistemological frameworks exclude marginalized resources. The remedy is to correct the biases that leads to the exclusion. Testimonial injustice is an illustration of first-order exclusion because credibility assessments lead to flawed knowledge. Second-order epistemic exclusion is when unwarranted identity prejudice leads to exclusions in the broader dominant resources resulting in a broad range of exclusions. The remedy is to include the necessary epistemic resources in the dominant framework. Fricker's hermeneutical injustice is a type of second-order epistemic exclusion.

Third-order epistemic exclusion, however, entails the inadequacy of an entire epistemic framework. Whereas first- and second-order exclusions can be remedied from within by making changes to or reforming the dominant system, even when those changes are made, third-level exclusions can still exist because of "the epistemic resilience of the system prevents new resources from outside of the episteme from altering the epistemic system" as a shield to avoid a "complete epistemic revolution."[35] The crucial point that Davidson makes is that by being overly focused on first- and second-order change, third-level epistemic oppression can remain intact. Davidson connects implicit bias research to being overly focused on first- and second-order epistemic change and ignores the radical change in the dominant epistemic system that is required for racial epistemic injustice to be remedied. Her point about the dangers of an exclusive focus on implicit bias that ignores the resilience of epistemic frameworks parallels the emphasis on the notion of willful ignorance and how it is sustained, discussed in the previous chapter.

Three additional and related limitations of diversity initiatives that are primarily based on implicit bias have been noted. First, the concept of bias is often understood to refer to automatic associations in the brain that facilitate individual functioning. Therefore, biases are often perceived as being hard-wired and, thus, an inevitable and a common, normal feature of human relations. Shirley Anne Tate and Damien Page[36] expose the dangers of presuming that bias is intrinsically within individuals. They note that when bias is assumed to be an inevitable and a normal function of the brain, and, thus, an inescapable consequence of living in a society, an exculpatory distance between the actor and the practice is implied. If everyone has biases, then "it's okay if I am (biased) too."[37]

A second concern with focusing on implicit bias as a remedy for social injustice is that it draws attention primarily to the individual. Being unaware of one's biases is considered a personal deficiency. This move obfuscates the ways in which institutional and systemic conditions enable individual bias and shield dominant epistemic frameworks from challenges. The focus on the individual—individual beliefs and individual behavior—can overshadow the ways in which subjects are connected to systemic structures and the ways in which power circulates through individuals[38] making subjects complicit in sustaining unjust systems.

Finally, and related to the earlier discussion, IBT assumes that those with bias can rid themselves of the attitudes that affect behavior if only they become aware of these beliefs and acknowledge their error. Even if this is possible, exposing implicit bias often ends with confession, as if awareness is all that is required. Confessing bias plays a key role in IBT. Yet, as already discussed in the previous chapter, confessions are problematic and often reinscribe injustice rather than challenge it. Because of this, Tate and Page insist that focusing primarily on unconscious bias is more than just limited—it is insidious. The allure of focusing on the unintended bias of individuals and the emphasis on confessing bias that is a result serves as an alibi for white supremacy and protects white innocence through enabling a will to ignore.

Building on Robin DiAngelo's[39] concept of white fragility, Tate and Page argue that a strong focus on implicit bias serves to reinstate white racial equilibrium that is disrupted when racism as a topic arises in discussions. White fragility, as DiAngelo defines it, involves a state in which even a minimum amount of racial stress becomes intolerable and, thus, triggers a range of defensive moves that reduce discomfort. When the focus is on the "unlearning" of bias that takes the form of confession, the emotional struggles of those with unconscious biases are recentered, and a form of self-forgiveness is produced that reduces feeling of guilt. When confession becomes the remedy for racism, it functions as a "fantasy of transcendence" where one is distanced from the very thing confessed. Moreover, confessing bias can become a performative act that allows one to believe that one has moved beyond racism. Fricker's remedy for epistemic injustice is not only limited but can reify injustice by recentering whiteness.

This digression into the critique of Fricker's overly individualistic solutions to correct for epistemic injustice helps to draw attention to what can be ignored by exclusively focusing on implicit bias or identity prejudice. Combating racial injustice requires understanding how institutional practices and unjust structures make racial injustice appear rational or reasonable. When the focus is on the individual, the situatedness of the individual in power structures can be ignored and the ways in which individuals are complicit in perpetuating systemic injustice can go unnoticed. Moreover, when one is exclusively focused on correcting individual instances of bias, one might also be encouraged to focus exclusively on the isolated event rather than the pattern of practices that the practices are an instance of. When unjust practices are considered in isolation, it is easier for them to be rationalized as insignificant slights rather than a part of an oppressive pattern of violence.

Marilyn Frye[40] offers a useful metaphor to help shift from an individual way of thinking to perceiving events as connected to larger structures of injustice. Frye distinguishes between oppression and other forms of suffering by explaining that the experience of oppressed people is

> that the living of one's life is confined and shaped by forces and barriers which are not accidental or occasional and hence avoidable but are systematically related to each other in such a way as to catch one between and among them and restrict or penalize motion in any direction.[41]

She introduces the metaphor of a birdcage to critique the microscopic perspective. If one were to examine the wires of the birdcage one at a time, one might not comprehend how that one wire is restrictive. It would seem like the bird could just fly around the isolated barrier to freedom. Yet, when one steps back, the entire cage that surrounds the bird becomes perceptible and it is perfectly obvious that the bird is surrounded by a network of systematically related barriers, no one of which would be the least hindrance to its flight, but which, by their relations to each other, are as confining as the solid walls of a dungeon.[42]

Oppression, therefore, involves a network of interrelated barriers that restrict the metaphorical movement of those inside the cage. When one is microscopically focused on only one wire of the birdcage, the macro-perspective can evade perception.

Expanding upon Frye, I submit that if one refuses to take a macro-perception then considering one's complicity in maintaining an unjust system can be escaped because the system remains undetectable. A refusal to perceive macroscopically is a form of willful ignorance, as discussed in the next section.

Fricker's analysis and remedy for epistemic injustice do not ignore macro-perspectives. Her analysis and remedy, however, do not adequately consider the relationship between the individual and the system. Thus, the role of complicity in the sense of willful ignorance and the ways in which such ignorance contributes to protecting unjust structures from challenges can go unheeded. In other words, the ways in which the defensiveness that dominantly situated individuals enact to deny their complicity in systemic injustice and the way the system in return supports that defensiveness is not only under-theorized but willfully overlooked in Fricker's project. Jose Medina's analysis of epistemic injustice and his suggested antidotes, however, do take willful ignorance seriously. The next section takes up Medina's recommendations for combating epistemic injustice.

EPISTEMIC FRICTION: TAKING WILLFUL IGNORANCE SERIOUSLY

Jose Medina[43] expands upon Fricker's work in significant ways. The starting point for Medina's understanding of epistemic injustice is his articulation of a specific form of ignorance which he develops in his depiction of the relationship between active ignorance and meta-ignorance described in the previous chapter. The type of "unknowing" that Medina attempts to correct for is more complicated than unawareness of identity prejudice. Recognizing that unknowing is the product of the systemic ignorance that Charles Mills propounds, Medina explains that socially sanctioned unknowing involves not only ignorance but also a numbness or insensitivity to insensitivity that he refers to as meta-ignorance. Meta-ignorance is actively perpetuated by individuals who benefit from the comfort of ignorance. As noted in the previous chapter, active and meta-ignorance have many parallels to what Pohlhaus and Dotson refer to as willful ignorance.

Although he focuses on virtues and vices, Medina recognizes that both virtues and vices are connected to social structures that reinforce them. Three epistemic vices that Medina claims generate meta-ignorance are epistemic arrogance (the tendency of "ruling without resistance"[44]), epistemic laziness ("a carefully orchestrated lack of curiosity"[45]), and close-mindedness (that creates "areas of an intense but negative cognitive attention, areas of epistemic hiding"[46]). These vices are "not incidental or transitory, but structural and systematic: they involve attitudes deeply rooted in one's personality and cognitive functioning."[47] According to Medina, these vices "inhibit the capacity of self-correction and of being open to correction from others."[48]

Medina argues that the epistemic vices he describes are mirrored in three corresponding epistemic virtues which he labels humility, curiosity as diligence, and open-mindedness. Following the work of standpoint theorists, Medina recognizes that marginally situated knowers are more apt to manifest these epistemic virtues than the dominantly situated knowers because they develop what W. E. B. Du Bois[49] has famously referred to as double consciousness from experiencing the violent effects of systemic white supremacy. While the epistemic vices tend to be generated by having the privilege of not knowing, not needing to know, and needing not to know, Medina insists that these vices are not exclusively attributes found in the systemically privileged. When found among the oppressed, however, such vices have different manifestations and different effects. Medina gives specific attention to understanding and remedying the form of ignorance that is a result of the structures of systemically privileged epistemology.

Following Linda Martin Alcoff,[50] Medina suggests that it is possible for dominantly situated knowers to develop a white double consciousness, although he expands this to what he refers to as "kaleidoscopic consciousness," a multiplicity of perspectives that are in constant epistemic friction with one another and that helps to cultivate epistemic virtues that can counter the vices. Polyphonic contextualism and kaleidoscopic perspectives create opportunities for the epistemic framework that one is embedded in to be challenged.

The tool that Medina champions for cultivating such the epistemic virtues that unsettle active and meta-ignorance is "epistemic friction." Kaleidoscopic consciousness involves the continuous exposure to and serious engagement with multiple and conflicting viewpoints that can produce productive friction and compels one "to be self-critical, to compare and contrasts one's beliefs, to meet justificatory demands, to recognize cognitive gaps, and so on."[51] Such internal and external-internal friction that leads to attempts to reach epistemic equilibrium among different and conflicting perspectives can, for

Medina, result in a meta-lucidity that acknowledges both the limits of what one knows and the relational aspect of such limitations. As Medina puts it, "Actively searching for more alternatives than those noticed, acknowledging them (or their possibility), attempting to engage with them whenever possible, and seeking equilibrium among them,"[52] functions as an antidote to meta-ignorance. Medina advocates real encounters with others or, at least, other perspectives that challenge one's world view.

Medina's emphasis on epistemic friction resembles the call for emotional trauma and discomfort in anti-oppressive pedagogies.[53] The trauma and discomfort provoked by epistemic friction are understood to be a crucial step in combating the arrogance of meta-ignorance. Medina, it must be noted, also acknowledges that without collective effort and major cultural transformations in our social imaginary, systemic ignorance will not be dismantled. In addition, Medina acknowledges that barriers to epistemic injustice are not exclusively cognitive but also affective. Medina emphasizes that epistemic justice will require transformations at the collective level as well as affective restructuring. The connection he makes with the affective dimension, though, is centered on developing empathy, compassion, and sympathy.[54] As is evident from the overview provided in the previous chapter, the empathy that Medina encourages the dominantly situated knower to cultivate must be vigilantly understood as also embedded in systems of power and oppression.

Some concerns, nevertheless, have surfaced around the call to seek out epistemic friction as a strategy for combating active and meta-ignorance and as a condition for building coalitions against oppressions. How does one steeped in meta-ignorance acquire the type of openness that Medina advocates? Can the recalcitrance of second-order meta-ignorance be penetrated by epistemic friction alone? Another way of putting this last question is: How can meta-ignorance be remedied when it is not perceived as a problem and, more specifically, when there are countless ways that epistemic friction can be avoided via socially sanctioned discursive practices? If exposure to others is already distorted by meta-insensitivities that are socially supported, how can exposure to alternative views be a remedy for meta-ignorance? What specific pedagogical practices can social justice educators introduce to rupture the defensive mechanisms of meta-ignorance? As Lori Gallegos de Castillo[55] notes,

> It is not entirely clear how to intervene upon the mutually reinforcing cycle of first-order and meta-ignorance. If exposure to others is distorted by meta-insensitivities, and if meta-insensitivities are confirmed by what one encounters, where precisely can we find hope for transformation? What specific practices, experiences, encounters, or educational approaches would disrupt the cycle of insensitivity?[56]

These questions must not remain unheeded because dominantly situated knowers can reproduce dominance in the process of seeking epistemic friction. Structures of domination continue to influence one's attempts to counteract ignorance. Thus, vigilance is key.

The call to opening oneself up to alternative perspectives prompts apprehensions that epistemic ignorance and innocence will be reproduced rather than challenged. The work of Melanie Bowman, Marianna Ortega, and Nora Berenstain each demonstrate, even when one engages and acknowledges other viewpoints, one can use that knowledge arrogantly or in ways that recenter white agency, consequently causing violence to the racially marginalized. Openness to other conceptual frameworks *without vigilance about how white innocence is protected* can produce a type of allyship that recenters whiteness and seeks moral absolution. Good white intentions, as noted throughout the chapters of this book, can be oppressive to people of color. The effects of good white deeds, consequently, are not only not transparent to white people but also unreliable. This is especially harmful when one believes one is absolved from responsibility because one engages with others' viewpoint and considers oneself to be "woke." Opening-up to alternative viewpoints alone will not help one work in solidarity with others if one is mired in moral arrogance.

Focusing on the systemically privileged who wish to act in anti-oppressive ways and who are aware of the limits of their own understanding, Melanie Bowman[57] advises caution when promoting the seeking out of epistemic friction because "the epistemic vices and cognitive distortions that created ignorance in the first place continue to influence knowledge-creation even after they are acknowledge."[58] Noting the circularity involved in the call for epistemic friction as a remedy to meta-ignorance, Bowman argues that "a person must be sensitive enough to see alternative viewpoints when they are present, which is one of the skills the profoundly meta-insensitive person lacks."[59] Calls for vigilance have been a recurrent theme in social justice education, in general, and critical whiteness studies, more specifically. Some representative examples of scholars across different disciplines who critically examine what it means to be white advocate cultivating vigilance as a response to white people's implication in systemic racial oppression.

In her discussion of the risks of reaffirming white moral agency in social justice education, Cris Mayo, for example, advances "perpetual vigilance" as a "necessary way to live one's life."[60] Vigilance involves a watchfulness and often implies that there is some constant danger that requires one to remain constantly alert. George Yancy, a prolific philosopher of race who uses phenomenology to expose the continued significance of race, advocates vigilance for the white antiracist because whiteness "is deferred by the sheer complexity of the fact that one is never self-transparent, that one is ensconced within structural and material power racial hierarchies."[61] Whiteness continuously "ensnares" and "ambushes" white people so that whiteness finds ways to hide "even as one attempts honest efforts to resist it."[62] Being an antiracist white, therefore, is a project that always requires another step and does not end in a white person's having "'arrived' in the form of an idyllic anti-racist."[63] This should not lead to hopelessness, Yancy insists, but rather "one ought to exercise vigilance."[64] Vigilance, according to Yancy, involves the "*continuous* effort on the part of whites to forge new ways of seeing, knowing, and being."[65] Sociologist Ruth Frankenburg unambiguously links the notion of criticality to vigilance when she pronounces that "(t)he *critical* examination of race, racism, and whiteness requires a particular kind of vigilance."[66]

Not only can epistemic vices prevent an individual from recognizing epistemic friction, but difficult and uncomfortable viewpoints can be reinterpreted in ways that do not seriously challenge dominant perspectives but, instead, replicate them. A well-cited illustration of such dangers is described by Mariana Ortega[67] who introduces the concept of "loving, knowing ignorance." Ortega coined the term to describe the stance of white feminists toward women of color who perceive themselves as progressives and want to learn about the experiences of women of color but fail to seriously engage with the knowledge of women of color and usurp their agency. Ortega exposes how the white perceiver believes herself to be perceiving the other out of love. Such loving perception, however, remains a form of "arrogant perception" that does not check and question with women of color and, thus, risks distorting their knowledge and/or using it for self-aggrandizing purposes. When they read and cite the work of women of color, white feminists claim to being open to "otherness," yet as Ortega demonstrates, because whiteness continues to shape white feminists' views, their perception of women of color's testimony and scholarship is arrogant. These white feminists appropriate what they learn for their own needs and desires in ways that reproduce injustice. White feminists, therefore, often seek out epistemic tension and yet still protect their white innocence.

Similarly, Nora Berenstain[68] critiques a type of openness to others that she describes as epistemic exploitation. Berenstain notices a pattern of practices and expectations in which the systemically privileged expect, and feel they are entitled to that is, that the racially marginalized should educate them about the nature of oppression and to prove that the systems that oppress them exist. As Berenstain underscores, epistemic exploitation is not perceived as such by the perpetrator. In fact, it is seen as a virtuous gesture: "I want to learn about you." As Berenstain notes, to the systemically privileged, epistemic exploitation "masquerades as a necessary and even epistemically virtuous form of intellectual engagement, and it is often treated as an indispensable method of attaining knowledge."[69] Such demands are perceived by the systemically privileged as normalized practices that are related to the seeking of truth: "exercising harmless curiosity," "just asking a question," "making a well-intentioned effort to learn," "offering alternative explanations," and "playing devil's advocate." Berenstain explains that "these innocuous euphemisms all help to mask the oppressive power dynamics at play in instances of epistemic exploitation."[70]

While systemically privileged individuals ostensibly want to be open to new perspectives, Berenstain exposes three harms that result from epistemic exploitation: (1) the unremunerated labor that the marginalized are expected to perform when put in a position to educate the systemically privileged, (2) the double bind that the marginalized must negotiate when put in the position to education, and (3) the additional exhaustion and frustration the marginalized experience when faced with the systemically privileged individuals' response of default skepticism when marginalized person decide to educate. The first harm involves the fact that when marginalized are compelled to educate about their experiences with oppression their labor will be "financially uncompensated, time-consuming, and mentally draining."[71] The second harm entails the double bind that is produced by the demand to educate. If the marginalized person refuses to educate, then she will be considered rude, shirking her duty, or being painted as unfriendly and aggressive. If the marginalized person gives into the pressure to educate, then she is not only forced to provide uncompensated labor but they will likely experience "racial battle fatigue," or social and psychological stress responses[72] (that result from trying to explain/prove the realities of structural oppression to those who dismiss and invalidate what the marginalized say).

This leads to the third harm that Berenstain addresses, the "default skepticism of the privileged."[73] Crucial to this account of epistemic injustice is that the skeptic positions him/herself as "the epistemic peer of the person of color with respect to this particular domain"[74] and, thus, skepticism seems to him/her to be merely a legitimate objection.

In her discussion of "privilege-preserving epistemic pushback," Alison Bailey[75] demonstrates how such discursive moves can pass as virtuous critical thinking when, in fact, it is a manifestation of willful ignorance and this sometimes makes it difficult to detect. Yet, such discursive patterns of response have harmful psychological and epistemic effects on marginally situated knowers. For example, in a discussion about rape, a male cis-gendered student might comment that men are victims too. The common rejoinder to Black Lives Matter, "All lives matter," is another illustration of default skepticism. A student who in discussions about white privilege says, "I'm just playing Devil's Advocate. Where is the evidence?" again, is an example of such default skepticism. Bailey explains that because the speaker considers this critical engagement, this pushback is perceived as a legitimate objection to an argument. However, she underscores that

> treating privilege-preserving epistemic pushback as a form of critical engagement validates it and allows it to circulate more freely; this...does epistemic violence to oppressed groups.[76]

Returning to Berenstain, when the educator treats what Bailey refers to as privilege-preserving epistemic pushback as if it were just a disagreement then not only does the educator forfeit the opportunity to discuss what the discursive practice does, it also allows the violence that marginally situated knowers experience in the classroom to go without challenge.

This brings Bailey to recommend a valuable pedagogical tool to disrupt such evasive strategies—treating them as "shadow text." Shadow texts can be unsettled by shifting the focus on what those discourses do and away from the literal and intended meaning of the utterance. Focusing on shadow texts makes explicit how epistemic resistance is reified in the classroom and can redirect the conversation in productive ways.

Finally, an additional way that seeking out epistemic friction by encountering others may reproduce injustice but appear to be engaging critically is what Ian Werkheiser[77] refers to as weaponized asking for reasons, already mentioned in the previous chapter. Ian Werkheiser argues that asking for reasons in the context of systemic injustice can be a weapon and sustain ignorance. Demanding reasons can result in epistemic violence and serve as a way for failing to provide uptake of marginalized knowledge. Recall that Wekheiser points to a conversation between Audre Lorde and Adrienne Rich. Lorde is disturbed by Rich's constant asking for evidence of what Lorde says. Rich explains to Lorde that when she is asking for "documentation," she is making a request to help her understand what Lorde is saying and not being dismissive of Lorde's ideas. Lorde, however, explains that the request for documentation is experienced as communicating doubt about what she said. Because of the pattern of default skepticism that marginally situated knowers expect to encounter, asking for reasons can be weaponized, especially when the criteria for justification are embedded exclusively in the dominant framework of intelligibility. Power continues, consequently, to lie in the hands of the dominant and dominant interests are recentered.

Asking for reasons becomes weaponized in the story that Dotson relates about Cassandra Byers Harvin, also mentioned in chapter 2. Harvin describes her need to avoid conversations about race with her white friends and colleagues because she can no longer deal with their hurt, surprise, and defensiveness.[78] Harvin relates an experience she had with a white woman in the public library who asked Harvin what she was working on. When Harvin explains that she is doing research on "raising black sons in this society," the white woman promptly inquires, "How is that any different from raising white sons?"[79] This asking for reasons may have been considered benign interest to the white woman but, as Harvin underscores, the white woman's question not only expressed a level of ignorance of the difficulties of raising a Black son in a white supremacist society but also that the tone, the skeptical manner, with which the question was framed implied in a condescending way that Harvin is "making something out of nothing."[80] Harvin chooses not to engage with the white woman and politely makes up an excuse that she is late and needs to leave the library: this was a conversation she could not have.

These scholars demonstrate that when the systemically privileged ask to be educated but then fail to utilize and seriously engage with what they are told, the active ignorance of the dominantly situated is maintained and dominant epistemic frameworks are protected from challenges—all under the guise of the pursuit of knowledge. And this can reverberate even when someone like Rich honestly wants to understand. While Medina's emphasis on epistemic friction entails serious engagement and is an important insight, these scholars show the complexity of even well-intentioned engagement and how being embedded in whiteness can make such engagement to go awry.

The effects of good white intentions are specifically detailed by Berenstain. She acknowledges the disproportionate pressure experienced by the marginalized to respond to the demand to educate. She highlights how emotionally exhausting it is to have to constantly justify and substantiate one's understanding of one's experience to those who do not have "the ears to hear."[81] Epistemic exploitation, Berenstain emphasizes, also keeps the marginalized busy with the needs and interests of the systemically privileged, and even more so when the latter remain skeptical of what the marginalized are trying to say. Because they refuse to entertain the concepts that the marginalized employ to articulate their experience (Berenstain) or even when they do not refuse but engage in ways that recenter whiteness (Ortega), the systemically privileged set the terms of the debate.

In her discussion of willful hermeneutical ignorance, Gaile Pohlhaus Jr.[82] offers some guidance for the type of engagement with conflicting views that may challenge such ignorance. She notes that

> when one genuinely cares to know something about the world as experienced from social positions other than one's own, one must use epistemic resources suited to (and so developed from) those situations. Prerequisites for acquiring such resources are, first, to allow the resources to be well-developed by persons situated in them; second, to trust those persons have developed them well, and third, to take an interest in learning to use those resources.[83]

White willful ignorance is an obstacle to the fulfillment of such prerequisites. Perhaps that is why Bowman strongly recommends that those who wish to act in anti-oppressive ways must *first* learn about "the provenance of their own ignorance of oppression"[84] and "understanding its purpose."[85] The necessity for such vigilance, for Bowman, derives from complicity. The arguments in this book attempt to draw attention to a particular type of vigilance that entails the recognition of how structures of domination continue to influence good intentions and obscure the harmful effects of such intentions in ways that reproduce rather than disrupt systemic racial oppression.

In a forcefully, insightful statement, Medina[86] offers that

> part of what needs to happen to counter the protective mechanisms of privilege is to make painfully visible the price of comfort under conditions of oppression, so that people cannot avoid the realization that the comfort of some comes at the cost of the discomfort of others.[87]

How can the effects of the price of comfort be acknowledged? Can cultivating a trait or virtue of open-mindedness facilitate such recognition? Open-mindedness is another virtue underscored by Medina as a remedy for the vices that lead to meta-ignorance. Is open-mindedness a remedy for systemic injustice? Although open-mindedness has been addressed since the late 1980s, notably by philosophers, in general, and philosophers of education, more specifically, recently there has been renewed attention to this concept. This scholarship is examined in the ensuing section.

THE CALL FOR OPEN-MINDEDNESS: A REMEDY FOR SYSTEMIC INJUSTICE?

Medina advocates cultivating the virtue of open-mindedness required for productive epistemic friction and for remedying active and meta-ignorance. The concept of open-mindedness is no stranger to philosophers of education who have debated and expanded our understanding of the meaning and value of open-mindedness as an intellectual virtue that serves as an aim of democratic education. Moreover, questions about the meaning, value, and limits of open-mindedness have been discussed by virtue epistemologists. Brilliant as their analyses have been, these accounts are limited in the context of social and epistemic injustice.

William Hare,[88] one of the pioneers in this area, contends that open-mindedness "involves a willingness to form and revise one's views as impartially and as objectively as possible in light of available evidence and argument."[89] Open-mindedness, thus, involves a willingness to form and revise one's beliefs on the grounds of available evidence derived from arguments that are objective and impartial. Hare's emphasis on evidence and argument is crucial to the type of criticality necessary for reaching an equilibrium between opposing viewpoints. As Hare puts it, "Open-mindedness . . . means being critically receptive to alternative possibilities, to be willing to think again despite having formulated a view, and to be concerned to defuse any factors that constrain one's thinking in predetermined ways."[90]

Hare's account of open-mindedness has been expanded as well as critiqued. What is the open-minded person open-minded about—beliefs, perspectives, oneself? What are the limits of open-mindedness? Does open-mindedness require belief-indifference toward one's own belief or can one hold a firm belief yet also be open-minded about it? These are some of the issues that have occupied scholars in this area. For instance, in his excellent book *The Inquiring Mind*,[91] Jason Baehr famously underscores that

> an open-minded person is characteristically (a) willing and (within limits) able (b) to transcend a default cognitive standpoint (c) in order to take up or take seriously the merits of (d) a distinct cognitive standpoint.[92]

Baehr's concern with cognitive standpoints intimates that open-mindedness is about perspectives that the individual has deep investments in. Moreover, reference to cognitive standpoints underscores that open-mindedness is not just about being open-minded toward every different perspective, belief, or idea. For instance, Baehr maintains that an open-minded person will only consider alternative perspectives when there is evidence to believe that doing so will lead to truth. Jack Kwong[93] interjects that genuine open-mindedness requires giving new ideas serious consideration or engagement but that open-mindedness entails the ability to determine when it is appropriate to be open-minded about an idea or perspective.

Wayne Riggs[94] offers that open-mindedness is epistemically valuable and can be consistent with having committed beliefs because open-mindedness is primarily an attitude toward oneself as a believer, rather than an attitude toward a particular belief. For Riggs, open-mindedness is characteristically an awareness of one's fallibility as a believer, that is, an acknowledgment that one can be wrong. Under this account, being open-minded does not require doubting one's commitment to a belief. Rigg's interpretation, instead, makes a connection between the call for open-mindedness and epistemic humility, a point that will be subsequently taken up with more specificity.

While brief, what this overview of some of the accounts of open-mindedness (selected from a huge body of scholarship) makes clear is that traditional analyses of open-mindedness put an intense emphasis on truth, evidence, impartiality, and objectivity. This leads Lauren Bialystok and Matt Ferkany[95] to critique what they point to as the presumed subject underlying traditional accounts of open-mindedness. According to Bialystok and Ferkany, the traditional accounts of open-mindedness take for granted a subject who is a rational agent who can impartially assess different viewpoints or beliefs on the basis of sound evidence. Moreover, it is a subject who is presumed to be willing to change an original perspective when there is rational evidence to do so. In another essay, Bialystok writes in astonishment about Hare's definition of open-mindedness that there are "a breathtaking number of assumptions in (Hare's) definition—the meaning of 'sound,' the definition of 'evidence,' and the possibility of relative objectivity or impartiality, to name a few."[96]

As the research on willful ignorance continues to expand, the need to problematize the criteria of determining truth becomes sharper. If dominant frameworks are maintained by making dominant resources seem reasonable to dominantly situated knowers (as discussed in chapter 2), what does this mean for the conceptualization of open-mindedness? Bowman, as already noted, argues that epistemic vices and cognitive distortions continue to influence dominantly situated knowers even when they are willing to seriously engage with different epistemic frameworks. George Yancy contends that dominantly situated knowers cannot transcend their positionality. What would this mean for conceptualizations of open-mindedness and what are the implications for education? Recent essays by philosophers of education offer reconsiderations of traditional analyses of open-mindedness that take up these challenges.

In an enormously valuable essay, Troy Richardson[97] reminds us that conceptualizations of open-mindedness must not ignore the ways in which dominant structures exclude alternative frameworks of intelligibility or the ways in which those dominant structures are shielded from critique. Traditional philosophers of education and virtue epistemologists who address open-mindedness overlook white ignorance, which, as Charles Mills contends, is a pervasive and systemically sanctioned ignorance in which white people misunderstand and misrepresent matters of race. Whites, Mills maintain, "*mis*interpret the world' and 'learn to see the world wrongly'"[98] and will often go to astounding extremes to deny what the racially marginalized say about their experiences resulting from systemic white supremacy. Moreover, such dominant frameworks of intelligibility have built-in defense mechanisms that can conceal oppression under the guise of rational assessment, as already noted. Mills compellingly demonstrates that whites have learned to see the world wrongly but with the assurance that these erroneous ways of perceiving the world will be validated by white epistemic authority.

According to Richardson, it is the dominant framework itself that requires disruption. Richardson focuses on the structure of settler colonialism that on no traditional account of open-mindedness is acknowledged. Richardson draws attention to the ways in which systems of dominance, privilege, and oppression remain unrecognized in traditional accounts of open-mindedness. Such accounts, thus, contribute to keeping such unjust systems protected from challenge. In a way, when it comes to dominant intellectual frameworks, traditional accounts evade critical assessment of the truth and evidence they claim to care about and forsake the very open-mindedness that they advance. Ironically, these accounts fail to be open-minded about the exclusionary aspect of dominant frameworks of intelligibility.

Two points stand out in some of the recent critiques of traditional analyses of open-mindedness that address this problem. First, these analyses of open-mindedness reassess the understanding of the subject that is presumed. Tadashi Dozono and Rebecca Taylor,[99] for example, underscore that traditional accounts assume a sovereign rational subject that is decontextualized and disembodied in the sense of being abstracted from the sociopolitical contexts and power dynamics they are embedded in. They explicitly underscore that traditional accounts of open-mindedness neglect to address issues of power or, in the words of Dozono and Taylor, "the role of social context or of the subject position of the individual open-minded agent."[100] Similarly, in her discussion about the differences between open-mindedness and epistemic vulnerability, Ann Chinnery[101] highlights that the former derives from a conception of subjectivity characterized by sovereign rational autonomy whereas the latter, as reinterpreted by Erinn Gilson, is grounded in a subject that is relational and inescapably dependent on the other. This is key to understanding open-mindedness in the context of teaching about social injustice.

Second, traditional approaches to open-mindedness presume that what it means to care about truth and what is considered sound evidence is incontestable and conclusive. As discussed in the previous chapter, when positionality is taken seriously and complicity in structures of power and privilege is not ignored, it becomes clear that open-mindedness must also apply to the ways in which reason and rationality can function to shield dominant epistemic frameworks from challenges.

Dozono and Taylor are unambiguously concerned with the challenges that K-12 teachers face when they teach about social justice to a diverse classroom of students. Some of the dilemmas that teachers encounter require that we ask: What account of open-mindedness should guide teachers? How should teachers respond to their own knowledge limits? Finally, and most significantly, what kind of authority can teachers exercise within a pedagogy of open-mindedness and within the context of legacies of epistemic injustice?

The remedy for epistemic injustice, they contend, requires more than open-mindedness. Other virtues like intellectual humility must supplement the cultivation of open-mindedness. Humility not only involves an acknowledgment of the limits of what one can know but must also take care not to recenter power and privilege. To counter such recentering requires a humility that recognizes the possible harmful effects of one's good intentions and requires the presumption of a subject that is relational. For Dozono and Taylor, the conception of open-mindedness that teachers enact must acknowledge the teachers' and the students' positionality and the ever-present complicated power dynamics in the classroom. They emphasize that teachers must not resist considering their complicity in "legacies of epistemic injustice" so that they can design lessons and their own pedagogy in ways that do not reinforce harm.

My insistence that dominantly situated educators recognize the ways in which their good intentions may obscure the harmful effects is apparent in the hypothetical story that Dozono and Taylor relate. A white teacher wanted to foster open-mindedness in her student during a lesson that focused on current manifestations of the civil rights movement. She anticipates that her students will debate competing views but will confirm her conclusion that current-day issues are an extension of past political movements for civil rights. Her intentions are good, yet she does not account for the way power circulates in her classroom or her own positionality. The teacher never considers that debating competing viewpoints around social justice issues can be experienced as violence to students whose viewpoints are marginalized in the larger social context. Moreover, the white teacher arrogantly takes for granted that she knows how students identify and she superciliously assumes what political stance the student holds based on her identity ascriptions. When the teacher brings up a discussion of women's rights, she finds it difficult to comprehend why a Black girl in the class withdraws or why her student is uncomfortable with essentialized understandings of women that imply a universal woman that excludes her student's intersectional identity. The Black student withdraws and stops speaking up in class.

People of color often withdraw from dialogue with white people who are attached to ignorance that excludes, marginalizes, and often tries to assimilate differently situated others into dominant worldviews. Moreover, when members of oppressed groups call attention to practices that limit their participation in dialogue, *they* are labeled the problem. Withdrawal can be a form of self-preservation, as well as a form of resistance, within a hostile environment where social inequalities are sustained and reproduce under the guise of good intentions.

Like Richardson, Dozono and Taylor recognize that education takes place within a colonial state, which impacts the type of open-mindedness that can be fostered in the classroom. They propose that teachers must be willing to critically examine their own positionalities and gaps in knowledge. Yet more than just filling in gaps in knowledge, Dozono and Taylor argue that dominantly situated teachers must develop a type of humility that is aware of the effects of willful ignorance both regarding the curriculum that the teacher selects and the pedagogy the teacher employs. I submit that our understanding of humility must also include the critical examination of the effects of one's good intentions.

Dozono and Taylor introduce "a justice-oriented pedagogy of open-mindedness" that must account for

> the ways that teachers themselves are socially situated subjects and the ways students are socially situated in relation to the school and the teacher. One aspect of this pedagogy involves reconceptualizing the authority granted to students in the learning process.[102]

The question of teacher authority will be further addressed in the following chapter. For now, it is important to accentuate that a justice-oriented pedagogy of open-mindedness requires "continuous reflection and adaption"[103] highlighting the significance of vigilance. Being vigilantly open-minded is further elucidated in Ann Chinnery's discussion of vulnerability.

In her response to Jennifer Logue's call for epistemic vulnerability to counter systemic ignorance, Ann Chinnery ponders how epistemic vulnerability differs from open-mindedness. Her work summarizes some of the points already made in this chapter, Chinnery concurs that the open-minded person must be willing to revise or reject a belief or viewpoint that is countered by sound objections. Chinnery, however, draws attention to what is considered sound objections. She argues that a precursor of open-mindedness is a type of humility that acknowledges that knowledge is partial, and that human knowledge is fallible. It is a type of humility, Chinnery submits, that is grounded in vulnerability.

Applying Gilson's understanding of vulnerability as an openness to affecting and being affected by another person, idea, or viewpoint[104] to our understanding of humility, Chinnery demonstrates the advantages of such vulnerability-based humility over conceptions of open-mindedness. To articulate this, we need to say more about Gilson's revision of vulnerability. Gilson modifies our understanding of vulnerability by critically examining the ideal of invulnerability which she argues entails close-mindedness. According to Gilson, the ideal of invulnerability is a masculinist norm that is grounded in the need for mastery, and that consequently protects dominant intellectual frameworks from challenges.

Gilson begins her analysis by challenging the erroneous but common definition of vulnerability as something negative and to be avoided. Exposing the problematic ideal of invulnerability as a masculinist conception allows Gilson to offer a revised, more positive account of vulnerability that is inherently tied to relationality and intersubjectivity and is characterized by a specific type of openness to being affected and affecting in turn. It is not that Gilson denies these more negative associations, she emphasizes that they are only part of the meaning of vulnerability. Gilson recaptures the *susceptibility dimension* of vulnerability and turns it into something positive by accenting the intersubjectivity of our living with others.

On Gilson's account, being vulnerable is *not only* about weakness, but instead, about "ambivalent potential." As she puts it:

> Being vulnerable makes it possible for us to suffer, to fall prey to violence and be harmed, but also to fall in love, to learn, to take pleasure and find comfort in the presence of others, to experience the simultaneity of these feelings.[105]

This acknowledgment of being reciprocally open to the other has transformative power in that it can reshape our sense of self and open us to new possibilities and capacities for understanding.

Gilson explicitly ties the pursuit of invulnerability and the denial of vulnerability to epistemologies of ignorance that maintain systemic oppression and privilege. Open-mindedness grounded in a masculinist ideal of invulnerability and the arrogance of a sovereign subject risks maintaining systemic white ignorance.

If the impetus for ignorance is *an attempt to avoid what might unsettle us*, when we ignore, we are necessarily avoiding our own vulnerability. We ignore because to know might disturb us and even disempower us, rending us vulnerable. As Gilson explains, "A refusal to recognize historical context constitutes ignorance about race and facilitates an ignorant preservation of white privilege, which is simultaneously a way of remaining ignorant about oneself and one's share in that history."[106]

For Gilson, the ideal of invulnerability supports the ideal of control and mastery and, thus, invites *closure*.[107] In a powerfully insightful move, Gilson argues that invulnerability is a position that

> enables us to ignore those aspects of existence that are inconvenient, disadvantageous, or uncomfortable for us, such as vulnerability's persistence. *As invulnerable, we cannot be affected by what might unsettle us.*[108]

The ideal of invulnerability consists of the habits and practices through which invulnerability and false control are sought and undergirds willful ignorance that invites ethical and epistemic closure. Thus, Gilson's notion of vulnerability also entails a type of vigilance that is watchful of any tendency to avoid what might unsettle us and an alertness to what obstructs new possibilities from being considered so that such tendencies can be thwarted.

Ignorance of vulnerability, therefore, precludes us from appreciating the effects of our practices on others and from acknowledging our complicity in the oppression of others. Fostering vulnerability, in contrast to adhering to the ideal of invulnerability, encourages those from dominantly situated positionalities to be open to marginalized views and to having dominant frameworks challenged. In other words, valuing vulnerability involves acknowledging our relationality to others and our intersubjectivity. This conception of vulnerability also takes power dynamics and positionalities seriously. To be vulnerable in this way is a form of humility because the vulnerable self is aware of its dependence on others for understanding the social world and the place of the self in it. Moreover, such humility that forefronts relationality requires a decentering of the self and a shift toward the interests of others.

Employing this revised lens of vulnerability, Chinnery makes a compelling argument about how reason might not be an adequate tool to capture social injustice. She points to the phenomenological account that Yancy[109] provides his experiences of a Black man who walks down the street and hears the click, click, click of car doors locking and that constitutes him as someone to be feared. Chinnery rightly points out that

> the educative potential of his phenomenological account ought not to be measured by standards of objectivity and impartiality, but rather by its power to destabilize prevailing assumptions about everyday racial relations and about our own position and complicity in those relations.[110]

Being open-minded in the sense of valuing vulnerability in the context of social injustice, for Chinnery, requires more than the capacity to weigh evidence and argument, it requires us "to be open to that which might shatter our knowledge, our identities, and even our self-understanding as knowing subjects."[111]

Mirroring Richardson's argument about disrupting dominant structures, Chinnery draws attention to how what is considered "evidence" might be part of the problem. Moreover, a type of humility that values epistemic vulnerability is more than a personal and individual acknowledgment of fallibility but also an acknowledgment of how structural features shape our beliefs, our identities, and our practices. A vulnerable type of humility, and even more significantly for dominantly situated knowers, will attempt to disrupt willful ignorance that can distort and misinterpret what is understood as "evidence."

How can such epistemically vulnerable humility be cultivated? How can dominantly situated knowers be more open to the limits of their understanding when willful ignorance makes that difficult? As Bialystok prompts us to consider, "What if what I most need to take seriously is my understanding of what counts as 'taking something seriously'?"[112] While these scholars emphasize the need for open-mindedness to be open-minded to critiques of dominant epistemic resources and intellectual frameworks, and I believe rightly so, this chapter has also attempted to forefront disrupting white innocence.

Disrupting innocence is a prerequisite for unsettling ignorance because it can arrest the defensiveness that can obstruct what we consider. When white innocence is protected, defensiveness overcomes the need to consider what alternative perspectives can offer. In other words, for dominantly situated educators, unsettling ignorance requires recognizing the ways in which the effects of good white intentions might harm students of color and how this might not be transparent for dominantly situated educators. Both Donozo and Taylor, as well as Chinnery, raise important concrete challenges for white educators who teach about systemic white supremacy to racially diverse students. In the next chapter, some of those challenges will be addressed in more detail.

TOWARD A VIGILANTLY VULNERABLE INFORMED HUMILITY

What are some of the takeaways from this chapter that might guide white educators through some of the challenges of teaching about whiteness to a racially diverse group of students? I want to be clear. The project of this book is not to examine methods for cultivating the type of humility needed for combating social and epistemic injustice. Nor is the aim of this book to provide formulas for action. Rather, the main objective is to tease out insights from the scholarship examined that might offer guidance for negotiating the challenges encountered by white educators teaching about whiteness to racially diverse students.

This chapter began with an appeal to cultivating humility that requires an awareness of and avoidance toward recentering whiteness, white desires, and interests. However, another feature of humility quickly arose in the scholarship: owning one's epistemic limits. Unpacking what such humility might require, Bailey accentuates the relational dimension of humility and she appeals to Gilson's reconceptualization of vulnerability to argue that humility involves an "openness before someone."

Throughout the chapters, it has been shown that owning one's limits requires acknowledging the limits and dangers of good, white intentions because the effects of good, white intentions are often obscured by those intentions. The requisite humility must not recenter white interests and desires so that being open before someone does not remain mired in systemically privileged arrogance. The point emphasized is cultivating being more open to and less defensive about considering the effects of one's good intentions.

The dangers of individualistic remedies to social and epistemic injustice are exposed through the critiques of Fricker's account that fails to adequately consider unjust structures, and even more significantly, that ignores the ways in which individuals are complicit in and help to maintain unjust structures. Correcting for implicit bias or identity prejudice focuses on individual people's mental states and draws attention away from structural explanations of oppression and the active role individuals play in sustaining unjust structures. An exclusive emphasis on biased minds offers a way to ignore real lived oppression in the world and allows systemically privileged individuals to disregard the ways that they contribute to that lived oppression. Severing the connection between individual bias, events, and practices and the broader patterns of oppression, obscures the connections between individuals and the harms they produce and the unjust systems license. Concentrating on individual bias or isolated events and practices obstruct recognizing the ways in which bias, events, and practices are part of larger patterns that together protect systemic oppression and privilege from contestation. Recognizing how unjust structures work through individuals puts individuals in a better position to recognize the effects of the social categories that they and others belong to and how willful ignorance can normalize oppression through tropes of "reasonableness." Even such discursive moves as asking for reasons can be weaponized unwittingly by white people who are well-intentioned.

Vulnerability, in contrast to open-mindedness, has been shown to be a valuable lens through which to understand humility. Because open-mindedness can entail a close-mindedness regarding dominant epistemic frameworks, the emphasis on vulnerability is constructive. Gilson's concept of vulnerability exposes the limitations of focusing on open-mindedness as a remedy for epistemic injustice when open-mindedness remains stuck to the ideal of invulnerability, mastery, and decontextualized subjects. Keeping at the forefront the subject as relational and as intersubjective facilitates the acknowledgment of our dependence on others for understanding the social world and this can facilitate an awareness of the complicity of dominantly situated individuals in the oppression of others. Vigilantly vulnerable informed humility appeals to the decentering of dominantly situated knowledge, dominantly situated ways of interpreting the social world, and opens a space for attending to the needs and interests of the marginalized as they negotiate systemic injustice.

How might the white educator teaching about whiteness to a diverse body of students be guided by the discussion of a vigilantly vulnerable informed humility? Some guiding reflections include the following:

White innocence and white ignorance must be combated, focusing not only practices that perpetuate innocence and ignorance of white students but also those of the white educator.

White educators need to attend more to when whiteness is recentered in the classroom not only in their curriculum but also in their pedagogy. Am I recentering my white students' needs and interests? Am I recentering my own needs and feelings?

Recognize that race and racism is relational, how is the comfort of white students contributing to the oppression of students of color?

How can the focus be shifted away from good intentions and to what practices, utterances, and behaviors do?

The problem of focusing on individual events or people, bad intentions, or blatantly harmful actions risks ignoring the systemic context within which they arise. White educators must remember to consider the pattern within which what seems like an isolated event is part of a pattern in a larger system that maintains injustice. Such discursive practices occur over and over. It is in seeing their repetition and pattern that one has a better chance of understanding their cumulative effects.

How can white educators learn to recognize shadow texts and expose them instead of hesitating to confront them?

Most significantly, how can white educators take students of colors' educational needs seriously: What do they want and need to learn? How can you support them?

How can white educators echo marginalized concepts in ways that disrupt the default skepticism students of color experience from white students and especially because, as Dotson demonstrates, systemic white supremacy works by making systemic oppression seem justified and "reasonable"?

White educators must stay with their own discomfort and be vigilant in seeking out when their complicity is unseen. These reflections must not be done in isolation but guided by the works of scholars of color who live the effects of white people's good intentions. Indeed, this not a closed "list" of "things to do" or questions to consider but instead serve as ideas that I hope will invite further reflection and critique.

In her review of Medina's book, Gaile Pohlhaus Jr.[113] asks about philosophers,

> How might we describe the kind of knowing that is practiced by philosophers qua philosophers, including the philosopher who is the author of *The Epistemology of Resistance* and how might philosophy be practiced (or fail to be practiced) in ways that are epistemically responsible?[114]

The next chapter will ask similar questions for white educators: How might we describe the kind of knowing that is practiced by the white educator teaching about whiteness to racially diverse students and how might social justice education be practiced (or fail to be practiced) in ways that are epistemically responsible? What are the implications of the scholarship discussed in this chapter that can help guide white educators through some of the challenges they encounter as they remain implicated in their complicity?

NOTES

1. Stephen Brookfield, "Killing White Innocence: A Review of George Yancy's *Backlash: What Happens When We Talk Honestly About Race. Tikkun* April 23, 2018.

2. George Yancy, "Dear White America." *The New York Times* (December 24, 2015). (This letter is reproduced in Yancy's book, *Backlash*.)

3. Stephen Brookfield, "White Teachers in Diverse Classrooms: Using Narrative to Address Teaching About Racial Dynamics." In C. Scott and J. Sims (Eds.), *Developing Workforce Diversity Programs, Curriculum and Degrees in Higher Education* (Hershey, PA: IGI Publishing, 2016): 98–117.

4. Christopher Bridges and Peter Mather, "Joining the Struggle: White Men as Social Justice Allies." *Journal of College and Character* 16, no. 3 (2015): 155–168, 162.

5. I. J. Kidd, "Intellectual Humility, Confidence, and Argumentation." *Topois*, 35 (2016): 395–402; A. Tanesini, "Intellectual Humility as Attitude." *Philosophy and Phenomenological Research* 96, no. 2 (2018): 399–420.

6. Mark Alfano, Michael Lynch, and Alessandra Tanesini, *The Routledge Handbook of Philosophy of Humility* (New York: Routledge, 2021).

7. Julia Driver. "The Virtues of Ignorance." *Journal of Philosophy* 86, no. 7 (1989): 373–384; Julia Driver, "Modesty and Ignorance." *Ethics* 109, no. 4 (1999): 827–834.

8. Julia Driver, *Uneasy Virtue* (New York: Cambridge University Press, 2001).

9. Brian Robinson, "'I am So Humble!': On the Paradoxes of Humility." In *The Routledge Handbook of Philosophy of Humility*, 26–35.

10. Heather Battaly, "Can Humility be a Liberatory Virtue?" In *The Routledge Handbook of Philosophy of Humility*, 170–184.

11. Elizabeth Spelman, *Inessential Woman* (Boston, MA: Beacon Press, 1988): 12.

12. Dennis Whitcomb, Heather Battaly, Jason Baehr, and Daniel Howard-Snyder, "Intellectual Humility: Owning our Limitations." *Philosophy and Phenomenological Research* 94, no. 3 (2017): 509–539.

13. Ibid., 516.

14. John Greco, "Intellectual Humility and Contemporary Epistemology: A Critique of Epistemic Individualism, Evidentialism and Internalism." In *The Routledge Handbook of Philosophy of Humility*, 271–282.

15. Ibid., 271.

16. Alison Bailey, "On White Shame and Vulnerability." *South African Journal of Philosophy* 30, no. 4 (2011): 472–483.

17. Samantha Vice, "How Do I Live in this Strange Place." *Journal of Social Philosophy* 41, no. 3 (2010): 323–342.

18. Alison Bailey, "On White Shame and Vulnerability," 473.

19. Barbara Houston, "A Conversation Beyond Argument: On a Bridge Over Troubled Waters." *Philosophy of Education Society 1997* (Urbana-Champaign, IL: University of Illinois, 1998): 28.

20. Bailey takes the term from James Baldwin who wrote that his skin color must "operate as a most disagreeable mirror, and that a great deal of one's energy is expended in reassuring white Americans that they do not see what they see." James Baldwin, "White Man's Guilt." In *The Price of the Ticket: Collected Nonfiction 1948–1985* (New York: St. Martin's Press, 1985): 409. As cited in Bailey, *The Weight of Whiteness: A Feminist Engagement with Privilege, Race, and Ignorance* (Lanham, MD: Lexington Books, 2021): 94.

21. Alison Bailey, "On White Shame and Vulnerability," 478.

22. Erinn Gilson, *The Ethics of Vulnerability: A Feminist Analysis of Social Life and Practice* (New York: Routledge, 2013). Also see Erinn Gilson, "Vulnerability, Ignorance, and Oppression." *Hypatia* 26, no. 2 (2011): 308–332.

23. Miranda Fricker, *Epistemic Injustice: Power and the Ethics of Knowing* (Oxford: Oxford University Press, 2007).

24. Ibid., 91.

25. Ibid., 92.

26. Ibid. Also see Miranda Fricker, "Replies to Alcoff, Goldberg, and Hookway on *Epistemic Injustice.*" *Episteme* 7, no. 2 (2010): 164–178.

27. Ibid., 17.

28. Cheryl Staats, "Understanding Implicit Bias: What Educators Should Know." *American Educator* 39, no. 4 (2015–2016): 29–33.

29. Linda Martin Alcoff, "Epistemic Identities." *Episteme* 7, no. 2 (2010): 128–137.

30. Rae Langton, "Review: Epistemic Injustice: Power and the Ethics of Knowing." *Hypatia* 25, no. 2 (2010): 459–464.

31. Ibid., 462.

32. Mark Tschaepe, "Addressing Microaggressions and Epistemic Injustice: Flourishing from the Work of Audre Lorde." *Essays in the Philosophy of Humanism* 24, no. 1 (2016): 87–101; Shirley Anne Tate and Damien Page, "Whiteliness and Institutional Racism: Hiding Behind (Un)conscious Bias." *Ethics and Education* 13, no. 1 (2018): 141–155; Christina Friedlaender, "On Microaggressions: Cumulative Harm and Individual Responsibility." *Hypatia* 22, no. 1 (2018): 5–21.

33. Lacey Davidson, "When Testimony Isn't Enough: Implicit Bias Research as Epistemic Exclusion." In Benjamin Sherman and Stacey Goguen, eds., *Overcoming Epistemic Injustice: Social and Psychological Perspective* (New York: Rowman & Littlefield, 2019): 269–283.

34. Kristie Dotson, "Conceptualizing Epistemic Oppression." *Social Epistemology* 28, no. 2 (2014): 115–138.

35. Lacey Davidson, "When Testimony Isn't Enough." 271.

36. Shirley Anne Tate and Damien Page, "Whiteliness and Institutional Racism: Hiding Behind (Un)conscious Bias."

37. Ibid., 145.

38. Michel Foucault, "The Subject and Power." *Critical Inquiry* 8, no. 4 (1982): 777–795.

39. Robin DiAngelo, *White Fragility: Why It's So Hard for White People to Talk about Racism* (Boston, MA: Beacon Press, 2018).

40. Marilyn Frye, *The Politics of Reality: Essays in Feminist Theory* (Trumansburg, NY: The Crossing Press, 1983).

41. Ibid., 4.

42. Ibid., 5.

43. Jose Medina, *The Epistemology of Resistance: Gender and Racial Oppression, Epistemic Injustice, and Resistant Imaginations* (New York: Oxford University Press, 2013).

44. Ibid., 31.

45. Ibid., 33.

46. Ibid., 34.

47. Ibid., 30.

48. Ibid., 31.

49. W.E.B. DuBois, *The Souls of Black Folk* (Chicago: A.C. McClurg & Co. 1903).

50. Linda Martin Alcoff, *The Future of Whiteness* (Malden, MA: Polity Press, 2015): 168–170.

51. Jose Medina, *The Epistemology of Resistance*, 50.

52. Ibid., 78.

53. Ann Berlak, "Confrontation and Pedagogy: Cultural Secrets, Trauma, and Emotion in Antioppressive Pedagogies," in Megan Boler, ed., *Democratic Dialogue in Education: Troubling Speech, Disturbing Silence* (New York: Peter Lang, 2004): 123–145.

54. Jose Medina, *The Epistemology of Resistance*, 210.

55. Lori Gallegos de Castillo, "Review of José Medina's *The Epistemology of Resistance: Gender and Racial Oppression, Epistemic Injustice, and Resistant Imaginations, APA Newsletter on Hispanics in Philosophy* 13, no. 2 (Spring 2014): 15–17.

56. Ibid. 17.

57. Melanie Bowman, "Privileged Ignorance, 'World'-Traveling, and Epistemic Tourism." *Hypatia* 35 (2020): 475–489.

58. Ibid., 477.

59. Ibid., 479.

60. Cris Mayo, "Vertigo at the Heart of Whiteness." In *Philosophy of Education 2000*, ed. Lynda Stone (Urbana, IL: Philosophy of Education Society, 2001): 319.

61. George Yancy, "Whiteness as Ambush and the Transformative Power of Vigilance." In his *Black Bodies, White Gazes: The Continuing Significance of Race* (Lanham, MD: Rowman & Littlefield, 2008): 231.

62. Ibid., 240.
63. George Yancy, *Black Bodies, White Gazes*, xxii
64. Ibid.
65. Ibid., 231.
66. Ruth Frankenberg, "The Mirage of Unmarked Whiteness," In *The Making and Unmaking of Whiteness*, eds., Birgit Brander Rasmussen et al. (Durham, NC: Duke University Press, 2001): 73.
67. Mariana Ortega, "Being Lovingly, Knowingly Ignorant: White Feminism and Women of Color. *Hypatia* 21, no. 3 (2006): 56–74.
68. Nora Berenstain, "Epistemic Exploitation," *Ergo: An Open Access Journal of Philosophy* 3, no. 22 (2016): 569–590.
69. Ibid., 570.
70. Ibid., 571.
71. Ibid., 573.
72. William Smith, Walter Allen, and Lynette Danley, "'Assume the Position . . . You Fit the Description': Psychological Experiences and Racial Battle Fatigue Among African American Male College Students." *American Behavioral Scientist* 55, no. 44 (2007): 551–578.
73. Nora Berestain. "Epistemic Exploitation," 578.
74. Ibid., 579.
75. Alison Bailey, *The Weight of Whiteness: A Feminist Engagement with Privilege, Race, and Ignorance*.
76. Ibid., 64.
77. Ian Wekheiser, "Asking for Reasons as a Weapon: Epistemic Justification and the Loss of Knowledge." *Journal of Cognition and Neuroethics* 2, no. 1 (2014): 173–190.
78. Cassandra Byers Harvin, "Conversations I Can't Have." *On the Issues* 5, no. 2 (1996): 15–16.
79. Ibid., 16.
80. Ibid.
81. Alison Jones, "The Limits of Cross-Cultural Dialogue: Pedagogy, Desire, and Absolution in the Classroom." *Educational Theory* 49, no. 3 (1999): 308.
82. Gail Pohlhaus, Jr., "Relational Knowing and Epistemic Injustice: Toward a Theory of Willful Hermeneutical Ignorance." *Hypatia* 27, no. 4 (2012): 715–735.
83. Ibid., 731.
84. Melanie Bowman, "Privileged Ignorance," 485.
85. Ibid., 486.
86. Jose Medina, "Response to Beth Sperry, Chris Lowry, and Gaile Pohlhaus." *Social Philosophy Today* 30 (2014): 207–216.
87. Ibid., 213.
88. William Hare, *Open-mindedness and Education* (Montreal, QC: McGill-Queen's University Press, 1979): 9.
89. William Hare, *In Defense of Open-mindedness* (Montreal, QC: McGill-Queen's University Press, 1985): 3.

90. William Hare, "The Ideal of Open-Mindedness and Its Place in Education." *Journal of Thought* 38, no. 2 (2003): 3–10, 4–5.

91. Jason Baehr, *The Inquiring Mind: On Intellectual Virtues and Virtue Epistemology* (Oxford: Oxford University Press, 2011).

92. Ibid., 202.

93. Jack Kwong, "Open-mindedness as Engagement." *Southern Journal of Philosophy* 54, no. 1 (2016):70–86.

94. Wayne Riggs, "Open-mindedness." *Metaphilosophy* 41, nos. 1–2 (2010): 172–188.

95. Lauren Bialystok and Matt Ferkany, "Open-mindedness from the Public Sphere to the Classroom." *Educational Theory* 69, no. 4 (2019): 377–381.

96. Lauren Bialystok, "How Open Should Open-Mindedness Be?" *Educational Theory* 69, no. 4 (2019): 534.

97. Troy Richardson, "Open-mindedness in a 'Post-Truth' Era." *Educational Theory* 69, no. 4 (2019): 439–453.

98. Charles Mills, *The Racial Contract*, 18.

99. Tadashi Dozono and Rebecca Taylor, "Teaching for Open-mindedness: A Justice-Oriented Approach." *Educational Theory* 69, no. 4 (2019): 473–490.

100. Ibid. 475.

101. Ann Chinnery, "On Epistemic Vulnerability and Open-mindedness." Cris Mayo, ed. *Philosophy of Education 2013* (Urbana, IL: Philosophy of Education Society, 2013): 63–66.

102. Tadashi Dozono and Rebecca Taylor, "Teaching for Open-mindedness," 488.

103. Ibid., 489.

104. Erin Gilson. "Vulnerability, Ignorance, and Oppression." *Hypatia* 26, no. 2 (2011): 308–332, 310.

105. Ibid., 310.

106. Ibid., 320 (emphasis added).

107. Ibid., 313.

108. Ibid. (emphasis added).

109. George Yancy, *Black Bodies, White Gazes*.

110. Ann Chinnery, "On Epistemic Vulnerability, 65.

111. Ibid.

112. Lauren Bialystok, "How Open Should Open-Mindedness Be?" 534.

113. Gaile Pohlhaus Jr., "Resistance and Epistemology: A Response to Jose Medina's *The Epistemology of Resistance*." *Social Philosophy Today* 30 (2014): 187–195.

114. Ibid., 188.

Chapter 4

When White Educators Are Part of the Problem

Teaching about whiteness is complicated and messy. One of the unique challenges of teaching about whiteness to a racially diverse group of students is that the classroom dynamic becomes part of the course content. Classrooms are not detached from the larger social world and, thus, structural inequalities are never left at the classroom door but instead power and privilege are replicated in the classroom in myriad ways. Moreover, white educators do not transcend their whiteness when they teach about and interrogate whiteness with their students. In her discussion of white resistance against antiracist pedagogy, Carol Schick[1] discloses that "as a White woman, it would also be disingenuous on my part to separate myself from my White students."[2]

This chapter seeks to examine how white educators who teach about whiteness to a racially diverse group of students can reproduce whiteness in their attempts to teach about disrupting it. However, the focus is not just on white educators who teach about antiracism, generally, but more specifically, white educators who acknowledge their complicity in systemic white supremacy and aspire to be vigilant in combating social injustice. Chapter 2 reviewed Sara Ahmed's work in which she advises white people who study whiteness to "stay implicated in what they critique,"[3] a theme that reverberates in the scholarly work discussed in the preceding chapters. This chapter explores whether the scholarship considered in the earlier chapters can offer insights for white educators who teach about whiteness and aspire to stay implicated in what they critique.

An enduring struggle for educators teaching about whiteness to a racially diverse group of students is checking that the pedagogical needs and feelings of white students are not recentered. Recentering white students gives rise to whiteness being violently enacted and harmfully experienced by students of color. It would seem simple, then: just avoid recentering whiteness!

However, white students' learning about their complicity in racism involves a "self-masking phenomenon"[4] where attempts to educate white students about whiteness risks giving rise to the very injustice the white educator is trying to disrupt.

White students' learning about whiteness is often toxic to the educational needs and interests of students of color because white students reproduce whiteness *as they learn about whiteness*. Under the ideology of white innocence, many white students believe that racism is not a white problem. Racism, for them, happens somewhere else—it is not about me! Moreover, when discussions of race, racism, and whiteness arise, white desires to know can appear to the white educators as harmless exercises of curiosity or the pursuit of truth, as discussed in chapter 2, but often reproduce whiteness in the actualization of those ostensibly good desires.

Often a primary aim of courses that teach about systemic white supremacy is to help white students recognize the ways in which they enact whiteness through their daily actions. Recentering white students' need to learn about whiteness, however, sidelines how whiteness is experienced by students of color. Students of color, for example, might need and want to focus on surviving the sustained experience of institutional racism and healing from its violence, even the violence they experience in the classroom.

Students of color are not only sidelined, but as Nora Berenstain details in her discussion of epistemic exploitation, recentering white needs, white feelings, and white learning is insidious. Borrowing the celebrated words of Audre Lorde, Ann Chinnery[5] explains that recentering white students' needs, interests, and feelings results in keeping the marginalized occupied with the master's concerns. Students of color end up on the receiving end of the violence this reproduction generates in the classroom or what Chinnery refers to as the "burden of cross-cultural work at the expense of their own learning."[6] White students' need not to be challenged and white students' desires to protect white innocence have negative effects on students of color. Moreover, white discursive moves that hide behind good intentions are especially harmful for students of color, as discussed in previous chapters.

Recall that George Yancy emphasizes the relationality of race when he explains "as you reap comfort from being white, we suffer for being black and people of color . . . your comfort is linked to our pain and suffering."[7] Similarly, Robin DiAngelo and Ozlem Sensoy[8] contend that:

> In the context of cross-racial dialogues that are explicitly about race and racism, what feels safe for whites is presumed to feel safe for people of color. Yet for many students . . . of color the classroom is a hostile space virtually all of the time.[9]

In the PowerPoints that Stephen Brookfield uses for the workshop and classes that he teaches, there is a quote from Carina Maye that vividly expresses the experience of Black doctoral students in a historically white institution.

> I honestly have been having a hard time being in predominately white classes lately as people in this country realize, again, the issues that exist in America for Black people. . . . While she was giving her long spiel on her good work, I couldn't figure out where to place my feelings. I could see it from a mile away; I even prepped myself for it before the class. I prepared for THIS, but I still wasn't ready. Her actions were soooo predictable, well, to me. It was something I knew was bound to happen in a class placed right in the heart of the world grappling with whether or not Black lives matter. But still felt completely uncomfortable, sick. Now, I am not one to dim anyone's light, but all I felt like saying was, "oh, okay. That's cute. You want a cookie?" I couldn't help but think, "this is not something new, why is it new to you? Why are you just now having these conversations?" I do not know this woman and may never have a class with her again; however, I will always remember what she did and how it made me feel.[10]

This is corroborated by the pattern of experiences that Alison Jones describes regarded cross-racial dialogues. In her analysis of her students' journals after the course was separated by race for part of the time, Jones emphasizes that the way safety is implemented in racially diverse classrooms is not safety for all. Jones advocates separate spaces for learning, separating white students from students of color, at least for part of the course. While there is much merit in this recommendation, in most historically white universities, courses separated by race might not be feasible.

Similarly, Zeus Leonardo and Ronald Porter[11] confront the appeal to safety in social justice education because it results in a recentering of white students' (and educators') desire to avoid difficult conversations about race, about white complicity, and it legitimates white defensiveness. They concur with other scholars mentioned above concluding that

> for marginalized and oppressed minorities, there is no safe space . . . mainstream race dialogue in education is arguably already hostile and unsafe for many students of color whose perspectives and experiences are consistently minimized. Violence is already there.[12]

Leonardo and Porter offer additional advice. They recommend that the educator reframe the classroom as a space of risk where the comfort zones of white students are not protected and do not result in "a symbolic form of violence experienced by people of color."[13] They maintain that meta-dialogue can be employed to foster such a space of risk.

Like appeals to safety, other apparently commonsense pedagogical ideals and assumptions may also unwittingly recenter systemically privileged students' needs and leave systemically marginalized students with the burden to educate at the expense of their own learning needs. Chinnery,[14] for example, critiques the pedagogical assumption that students "ought to share their experiences with others, that they should do so willingly, and that they should tell the truth in these exchanges."[15] According the Chinnery, marginalized students are placed in a double bind. If they refuse to share their experiences, they are demonized for refusing to teach, for refusing to share the knowledge they have, for refusing to care, and for refusing to be grateful that they have been included. If they agree to share their experiences, however, they are often burdened with having to endure the default skepticism, so aptly described by Berenstain, that masquerades as virtuous learning—"I just want to know." In addition, when students of color are expected to carry the burden of educating white students, both white students and white educators feel exempt from doing their own work learning about their complicity in systemic white supremacy. Thus, not only do racially marginalized students not gain anything from cross-racial dialogues, they also endure the violence of white resistance, white denials, and the recentering white feelings.

The primary focus of this chapter, then, follows from the realization that how white educators respond to what occurs in the classroom is further complicated because the safety (more, explicitly, the comfort) of white students is incompatible with the safety of students of color. How do white educators who teach about whiteness to a racially diverse group of students and acknowledge their complicity in systems of power and privilege perform, normalize, and recenter whiteness in the classroom, even under seemingly "good" pedagogical practices? How does the white educator's investment in whiteness impact students of color, and protect the whiteness of education from challenges? How can white educators recognize how their own whiteness obstructs their ability to understand their students of color's educational needs? How do white educators teaching about whiteness to a racially diverse group of students negotiate their complicity? Since being white affects not only what one teaches but also *the way one teaches*, this chapter critically examines three pedagogical challenges that white educators who teach about whiteness report complicate how they respond and move forward with the class. Insights from the previous chapters will be drawn forth to suggest ways to understand and possibly address these challenges.

Cognizant that a focus on white educators yet again recenters whiteness, it must be first emphasized that examining white educators' challenges in teaching about whiteness in no way implies that these challenges are comparable to those encountered by educators of color. Cheryl Matias,[16] for instance, powerfully critiques the one-sided accounts of the painful lives of white educators who "*serve, help, or save* People of Color"[17] and elevate white pain above the pain of educators of color. As she powerfully describes the trauma of her own teaching,

> as a Brown-skinned, Pinay teacher educator from urban Los Angeles, I painfully attest that teaching in a White institution with White colleagues and White students is a trauma, one that relentlessly terrorizes my heart, soul, and psyche on a daily basis.[18]

Studies have demonstrated that faculty of color who teach courses around race and racism contend with reactions from white students that can range from incredulity to open hostility,[19] leaving faculty of color feeling exhausted by their classroom encounters. In addition, studies have shown how faculty of color also must deal with extraordinary resistance that is manifested in students' negative course evaluations that can impact their tenure and promotion cases.[20] Thus, when I describe the "challenges" that white educators encounter, it is not *the difficulty* of the challenge that is being given attention. Rather, the aim is to bring some of these issues out in the open so that white educators can become better at educating all their students.

Second, contemporary research on white professors' challenges in teaching about race and racism are mostly concerned with white student resistance.[21] The focus of this chapter is on white educators who acknowledge their white complicity and how might the insights discussed in the previous chapters aid white educators in negotiating that complicity. When white educators can better recognize how whiteness is being reproduced through their pedagogy, it becomes possible to create educational opportunities where racially marginalized students can engage in learning that confirms that their lives and experiences really matter. What would it mean for white educators to center the effects of whiteness on students of color? Can this combat the tendency for critical whiteness studies from becoming critical whiteness for white people only?

The three challenges addressed in this chapter are related. The first challenge critically addresses a common pedagogical assumption: teach students "where they are at." One consequence of white educators teaching white students "where they are at" entails *a hesitancy to challenge them* when they reproduce whiteness in subtle ways that are not visible to them yet. This leads to a second challenge that white educators may encounter related to an ambiguity experienced by the white educator around white students' learning and the violence it generates in the classroom. When white educators are uncertain about or have a difficulty with the distinction that Bailey describes between the literal interpretation of an utterance and what such an utterance does (its impact), they, as in the previous case, might hesitate to call out white students' discursive reproduction of whiteness in the classroom. Hesitating to critically challenge white students again segues into a third challenge. There are many studies that show white educators hesitate or refuse to challenge students of color and, thereby, possibly denying them critical feedback that they need to progress through their academic program.

Although much has already been published about white educators and their discomfort around teaching about race, racism, and/or whiteness, most of these studies focus on capturing white educators fear, their intimidation, and their expressed uncertainty around teaching about the realities of race, racism, and/or whiteness. This research is valuable. The challenges experienced by white educators teaching about systemic white supremacy that this chapter emphasizes, however, explicitly follow from the idea that white students' learning is toxic to students of color and that white educators' complicity must be vigilantly scrutinized. This chapter attempts to connect the bodies of scholarship in critical whiteness studies and epistemic injustice with the experiences of some white educators in the hopes that the insights from the scholarship can help white educators support more meaningful learning for all students.

BEGINNING WHERE THE STUDENT IS AT

In his discussion of the dynamics of teaching race, Stephen Brookfield,[22] a staunch antiracist white scholar who critically acknowledges that "to feel safe is my norm,"[23] suggests that it is important to "ease" white students into understanding their complicity in whiteness in a way that is not confrontational but instead invitational. His objective is to prevent white students from resisting and tuning out of the conversation. Brookfield *does not* discount the necessary role of discomfort for white learning but instead suggests that such discomfort be scaffolded.

In "The Dynamics of Teaching Race,"[24] Brookfield further advocates that educators begin teaching where the student is at. As the student begins to develop conceptual tools to recognize the reality of racism, and when they begin to trust their peers and their teachers, *then and only then* "the level of dissonance, contradiction, and discomfort can be ratcheted up."[25] At the same time, Brookfield is himself uneasy with his approach to teaching about race. When he advocates using personal narratives of transformation as a model for white students he ponders:

> Does this approach pay too much respect to white fragility, to the alarm and subsequent retreat from confrontation that stops so many of us from looking

squarely at our own racism? I go back and forth on this question. My teacher voice says, "you have to start where people are. Starting with your own agenda without having built a connection to their world is self-indulgent. Get over making yourself feel righteous and take the time to know them." My activist voice replies, "here you go again, copping out and backing off from necessary danger. Don't be so cowardly—tell it like it is."[26]

"White fragility," a term coined by Robin DiAngelo, describes the state in which "even a minimum amount of racial stress becomes intolerable, triggering a range of defensive moves."[27] Brookfield contemplates whether his easing into race talk with his students and whether his emphasis on modeling through personal narratives of transformation are forms of diversion that restore the comfort disrupted by explicit discussions of whiteness.[28] Is easing white students into learning a form of encouraging white students' learning or colluding with whiteness by appeasing comfort?

Brookfield is not alone in contending that white students' learning must start where the student is at. Ann Curry-Stevens'[29] model of transformative education for the privileged emphasizes that white students' learning about whiteness must be *slowly staged* and her approach takes the concept of white privilege as the starting point for such learning. Based on her empirical study of educators who engage in pedagogy with systemically privileged learners, Curry-Stevens advocates, "slowly staging the development of privileged learners so as to pay attention to their particular needs"[30] by introducing privileged learners first to Peggy McIntosh's work on the invisibility of the white unearned benefits and only then problematizing McIntosh's ideas for not going far enough.

Zeus Leonardo,[31] in contrast, contends that the starting point for teaching white students should be white supremacy/white domination and not white privilege. Leonardo defines white supremacy as the "direct processes that secure domination and the privileges associated with it."[32] According to Leonardo, white supremacy is the condition that makes systemic privilege possible. By existing and benefiting from white supremacy, white people are complicit in a system that oppresses people of color. Leonardo insists that white students' learning must begin with an acknowledgment of white people as active oppressors and perpetuators of unjust systems rather than begin with a focus on unearned privileges. The emphasis on the concept of white privilege, Leonardo maintains, encourages an assumption of white passivity buttressed by the notion of *unearned* white advantages. Subsequently, if the accent is on passively receiving privilege, the ways in which white people are currently, and perpetually, active agents in the maintenance of white supremacy/white dominance can be obscured.

The debate centers around the order of pedagogical emphasis because both Curry-Stevens and Leonardo agree that white students are to be taught to recognize the ways in which they are complicit in racial injustice even when, and especially when, white students have good intentions. Curry-Stevens, like Brookfield, believes that beginning with white supremacy can provoke resistance and risks "having the learners discredit the educator" and "imperil(s) the psyche to such an extent as to render the approach ineffective."[33] Leonardo recognizes that the advantage of white privilege discourse is that it encourages whites to be more receptive and limits white guilt (in fact, he tells us that he assigns McIntosh's article in his courses). Nevertheless, he is concerned that a concentration on privilege hides the ways in which whites play an *active* role in the domination of people of color.

This disagreement around how to teach about whiteness goes deeper because, as Leonardo contends, a critical analysis of whiteness is "best apprehended from the experiences or vantage point of the oppressed."[34] In other words, educators and researchers must analyze whiteness not from the recentered perspective of a white audience but from the objective experiences of those on the receiving end of oppression. This suggests that education about whiteness, regardless of whether or not it should begin where white students are at, must not ignore students of color as part of the equation.

What is the experience of students of color when their pedagogical needs are put on hold while white students are eased into learning? In chapter 2, Deanna Blackwell's[35] research, already noted, explores the ways in which Black students are sidelined when white students' needs are centered in anti-racist education. Blackwell explains:

> Are we to assume that students of color have already reached the pinnacle of race consciousness as a bodhisattva has achieved enlightenment; or that bearing witness to white race consciousness-raising is benefit enough? Anti-racist education, even in its attempt to uncover the subtleties of racism, continues to be preoccupied with white students at the expense of students of color.[36]

Blackwell's point is exceedingly significant in that it exposes a pattern of white educators sacrificing the opportunity to help students of color develop meaning around their own experiences with systemic white supremacy to address, and in hopes of realizing, white students' epiphanies. Blackwell also uncovers how students of color are marginalized when they are "often pressed to choose from a confining set of racial roles to play in college classrooms."[37] White teachers frequently position students of color as cultural experts, teacher's aides, or witnesses to white students' epiphanies. None of these roles address their own educational needs. Blackwell underscores the ways in which white students' learning often comes at the expense of the educational needs of students of color.

Moreover, the epistemic exploitation of students of color can generate racial battle fatigue or the stress from having to live in and navigate white spaces.[38] One of Alison Jones'[39] students of color writes in her journals that when they are in courses with white students,

> I prepared myself to argue any point I felt at odds with, with anybody not or a brown skin tone, to enlighten them upon the cultural ideals, values, and beliefs that didn't correspond to their own.[40]

When white educators do not disrupt white habits of diversion or postpone doing so because they want to ease white students into learning, students of color may feel they are compelled to speak up and challenge their white peers. Even if students of color decide to remain silent, they are often put in the position of having to yet, again, make a choice between speaking up and risk the hostile dismissals of white students or staying silent and enduring painful untruths go unchallenged.

In their critique of calls for safety mentioned previously, Zeus Leonardo and Ronald Porter describe the catch 22 students of color experience when they either must

> observe the safety of whites and be denied a space that promotes people of color's growth and development or insist on a space of integrity and put themselves further at risk not only of violence, but also risk being conceived as illogical or irrational.[41]

To have to deliberate these choices adds to the violence that students of color experience when white educators begin where white students are at.

Moreover, white students' pleas to be taught by students of color reify the very norms of whiteness that social justice pedagogy aims to disrupt because these appeals seem so virtuous. A discussed in chapter 2, Kristie Dotson[42] explains that epistemic injustice is reified through what seems reasonable and virtuous. Dotson[43] also shows how systemically dominant knowers' consistent refusal to give uptake to what marginally situated knowers say can lead to testimonial silencing and testimonial smothering.

Jones offers a powerful insight when she contends that white students' epiphanies give pleasure to progressive teachers which hints at why white teachers might desire to focus on white students' learning in the first place.[44] What is this pleasure that progressive white educators receive in recentering white students' learning? Does it assuage white educators' comfort when they are conflict-aversive? Do white students' epiphanies allow white educators to feel good about themselves reassuring their self-image as racially innocent? Fellows and Razak, whose arguments are addressed in chapter 2, remind white feminists that to begin the process of feeling less innocent they need to critically ask themselves:

Where have we positioned other women within our strategies for achieving social justice?
What do we gain from this positioning?
How are we implicated in structures of dominance?

I submit that when white educators are concerned with teaching where white students are at that it is important to reflect on:

How does this approach to teaching position students of color?
How does this approach benefit white educators? What would it mean to give up or combat one's desires for innocence?
How does the pedagogical approach or principle employed implicate white educators in the reproduction of structures of dominance not only by sheltering white educators' innocence but also by legitimating rather than challenging willful ignorance?

WAS THAT RACIST? WHEN DISTANCING STRATEGIES HIDE BEHIND AMBIGUITY

In May 2019, Doug Glanville, a former major league baseball player and currently a sports commentator, addressed an incident in which a fan wearing a Cubs sweatshirt stood behind him and made an upside-down "OK" sign with his hand. Glanville, who is Black, wrote an op-ed piece in the *New York Times*[45] explaining the ambiguity of the sign and its connection to racism. While the gesture could just simply indicate OK, most recently the sign has been co-opted to reflect support for the Alt-Right. Glanville emphasizes the ambiguous character of the gesture noting that "ambiguity has always been a friend to racism." Racism flourishes in ambiguity, in double meanings, and that is most likely precisely why white supremacists have adopted this sign, to begin with.

In the previous section, Stephen Brookfield was quoted as critically, self-reflectively questioning his own pedagogy, "Don't be so cowardly—tell it like it is." But what if "what it is" is not clear to the white educator? As a white educator, I am occasionally confounded by ambiguity that hides whiteness. Because white students learning about whiteness is violent to students of color, there are times I find myself wondering if a microaggression, a distancing strategy, or a white denial is occurring. In a class discussion, for instance, I might be unsure if a white student is asking a genuine question and making a comment necessary for his/her/their learning or displaying a discursive tool to recenter white innocence and white agency. And it could be both. Even being aware that this is how racism obscures itself to white people, I may still hesitate in my response to the white student.

During the beginning of class after the Black Lives Matter protests following the murder of Breonna Taylor at the hands of the police in her own home, one of my white students wanted to talk about her participation in the demonstrations. At first thought, this would not seem to be inappropriate. The course addresses issues of racism/whiteness and education. As she was speaking and taking the center stage, however, I began to wonder whether the white student's insistence to speak about her participation in protests was an illustration of virtue-signaling that should not remain unchallenged.

Recalling Kathy Hytten and John Warren's[46] ethnography demonstrating how whiteness gets reinscribed and protected through a variety of forms of strategic rhetoric even as educators attempt to disrupt whiteness' normative influence, these discourses can be employed both in enabling and disenabling ways. On the surface, a discourse may be a useful way of engaging and/or attempting to understand the experience of others. It becomes disabling, however, when the focus remains entirely on the self and when the discourse serves to avoid complicity.[47] Hytten and Warren offer the example of Randy, the only openly gay man in the class who is also white. In all his journals and often in class discussions, he forefronts his gay identity and rarely mentions his whiteness. Hytten and Warren recognize that his persistent reference to his sexuality highlights important intersections in their class discussions. It is only after he repeatedly avoids reference to his also being a white male, however, do they realize that his talk is disenabling and allows him to avoid considering the ways in which, as white, he is implicated in perpetuating systems of racial injustice. Until a pattern emerges of Randy being self-absorbed in appeals to his gayness, the white educators can seem uncertain whether his discursive utterances were enabling or disenabling.

As Glanville notes, ambiguity is a fundamental tool of white supremacy. This ambiguity is addressed in the scholarship that studies microaggressions. Derek Wing Sue defines racial microaggressions as the "brief and everyday slights, insults, indignities and denigrating messages sent to people of color by well-intentioned [people]who are unaware of the hidden messages being communicated."[48] When a woman clutches her purse in an elevator as a Black man enters, the message conveyed is that Black men are criminals. The woman may not intentionally clutch her person or consciously have an explicit belief about Black men and criminality. Yet, as George Yancy[49] so forcefully articulates, the ambiguity that characterizes her act allows one to doubt the racism behind the act. Yancy critically examines the many ways his experiences as a Black man in an elevator with a white woman can be misinterpreted as not about race, although he knows it is about race.

Asian-Americans born in the United States frequently report being asked by non-Asians: "Where are you really from?" At a literal level, this can seem like a reasonable question to ask a new acquaintance. The reasonableness of asking about a person's family background and place of birth, however, becomes problematic when this question is directed toward specific ethnic groups, and not to others, in *systemically patterned* ways. What the utterance does is send an implicit message that people with Asian background are not "real" Americans in the way that those who have European heritage are and that they do not belong here.

Attribution ambiguity is a characteristic of microaggressions that researchers have studied especially because of the harmful effects such ambiguity can have on the marginalized.[50] Marginalized group members not only painfully experience microaggressions but because microaggressions can be "explained away" by perpetrators and observers, the target of the microaggression can experience a secondary harm in feeling unsure about the racial message hidden behind the interaction as well as how to respond to it. The ambiguous nature of microaggressions can lead those who experience them to doubt their interpretation of the incident and the way they make sense of what is happening to them.

In her discussion of microaggressions and epistemic injustice, Saba Fatima[51] poignantly describes the consequences of experiences that because of attributional ambiguity cannot be clearly classified as racist. Attributional ambiguity, Fatima explains, is when "members of groups that experience social stigma find it challenging to determine whether the feedback they receive is based upon their personal deservingness or if it is discrimination against them because of their social identity."[52] Yet, as discussed in chapter 2, Fatima emphasizes that more often it is not that she is unclear that that racism is at play. The real problem lies in that there is no uptake of the words that she uses to describe her experience, and *this* can contribute to self-doubt and shake the ground of her perception of social reality. The discussion around epistemic injustice and willful ignorance in chapter 2 highlights not only many of the negative effects that the systemically marginally situated knowers experience when their testimony and when their intellectual frameworks of meaning are denied uptake by systemically dominant knowers but also how the systemically marginalized might justifiably choose to withdraw completely, whether physically or psychologically, from participating in discussions about race, racism, and whiteness.

Sometimes the tone of the utterance makes it is possible to discern white dismissals and white distancing strategies. Recall Dotson's reference to Cassandra Byers Harvin's response to the white woman who seems interested in her research project about raising Black sons. The woman asks Harvin in a dismissive and skeptical tone, "How is that any different from raising white sons?" Consequently, Harvin makes up an excuse and withdraws from the space because she knows this is a conversation she could not have. Would a white educator, however, have discerned that tone or thought it was just an inquisitive request? Again, only when the white woman's question is not considered an isolated act but instead an instance of a pattern of white women asking skeptical questions of women of color that the harm of the question becomes clear. There is a *patterned absence* of seriously engaged uptake.

The situation is more complicated because even without an attitude on the part of the white woman asking the question, being asked for reasons can still be weaponized. Recall the conversation between Audre Lorde and Adrienne Rich in chapter 2 where Lorde explains that Rich's request for "documentation" to aid her understanding is experienced by Lorde as expressions of doubt and incredulity because of the pattern of default skepticism and lack of seriously engaged uptake that she has consistently encountered from white women.

White educators who teach about whiteness might be able to recognize that microaggressions cannot be understood as isolated events. We have studied the ways that ambiguity can be minimized when microaggressions are connected to larger patterns of unjust practices. Still, it might be especially challenging in certain cases for the white educator to discern when white students are performing distancing strategies, especially when those discursive moves hide behind ostensibly good intentions.

I return once again to Ahmed's response to white students who ask, "But what should white people do?" and discussed in chapter 2. Ahmed[53] acknowledges that at first sight, the asking of this question might seem like progress,

> it can be an impulse to reconciliation as a "recovering" of the past (the desire to feel better); it can be about making public one's judgment ("what happened was wrong"); or it can be an expression of solidarity ("I am with you"); or it can simply be an orientation towards the openness of the future (rephrased as: "what can be done?").[54]

However, even if this question can seem at first to be, to borrow Hytten and Warren's terminology, enabling discourses, it can function as a disenabling discursive move because it does something above and beyond the literal interpretation of the words. As Ahmed continues to explain:

> But the question, in all of these modes of utterance, can work to block hearing; in moving on from the present towards the future, it can also move away from the object of critique, or place the white subject "outside" that critique in the

present of the hearing. In other words, the desire to act, to move, or even to move on, can stop the message "getting through."[55]

Ahmed's caution serves to underscore the way that ambiguity of a simple, seemingly benign, and well-intended question—"But what should white people do?"—functions as a rhetorical tool to derail discussion, silence critique, and to dismiss voices of color in the classroom. Instead of being stuck on the ambiguity of intent, Ahmed urges whites to focus on the effect. In this case, the questions "But what should white people do?" can obstruct the type of listening that is required to genuinely engage with the question.

Despite years of studying how white ignorance is actively managed[56] by such ambiguity and in spite of knowing that I need to switch to a macro-perspective[57] in order to recognize a microaggression and its harm, I sometimes hesitate to respond in a way that would disrupt a white student's comment/question because I am uncertain whether the utterance is enabling or disenabling. My students of color, on the other hand, who have implicit knowledge[58] and who may know things from a lifetime of first-hand experience, might not have time or patience for my processing what happened and any delay in disrupting what the white student is doing constitutes further violence to their learning. Students of color at predominantly white institutions not only battle institutional racism and microaggressions from white students in their classrooms but are also harmed when white professors remain silent in face of the microaggressions students of color endure in the process of white students learning about their whiteness.

To return to the story of my white student who insisted on discussing her presence at the Black Lives Matter protest, the insights I glean from the scholarship in preceding chapters help me to recognize that the ambiguity matters less than what her discourse might be doing. Given what Leonardo tells us about the tool of meta-dialogue and what Bailey offers about exposing shadow texts, a possible response in this case would be to immediately raise a question about how the media coverage of the Black Lives Matter protests was different when the focus was on white demonstrators. Rather than a diversion, this can be a way to avoid further recentering the white student discourse while also not ignoring its effects. Providing an essay that critically examined the media attention on the unprecedented white support in these protests can open a space for rich discussion. Introducing the concepts of virtue-signaling and performative allyship also seems relevant and useful.

I steer clear of providing formulas or lists that tell white educators what to do when the uncertainty of ambiguity confounds them. Instead, I invite critical feedback around the suggested response to this incident of ambiguity and encourage other ideas for dealing with this challenge. In this chapter, my aim is to demonstrate what the insights of the scholarship reviewed in the previous chapters can offer. Instead of getting stuck in trying to clear up ambiguity that is embedded in seemingly good intentions, focusing on the effects of disenabling discourse may offer ways to open up opportunities for making the class a space of risk and to transform disenabling discourse into enabling situations. Staying alert for the effects of white discursive moves in our pedagogy and not being baffled by what seems ambiguous can help white educators make constructive pedagogical moves before students of color feel compelled to speak up and educate. As one student of color in my class once exhaustingly exclaimed, "I am not getting paid to teach white students."

GIVING CONSTRUCTIVE CRITICAL FEEDBACK TO STUDENTS OF COLOR

In chapter 1, John McWhorter's critique of the white complicity claim that is a core element of critical whiteness studies was examined. The idea that all whites are racist, according to McWhorter, "has white Americans muzzled, straitjacketed, tied down, and chloroformed for good measure."[59] McWhorter insists that the white complicity claim silences white people because anything one says can be interpreted as racist. The fear of being accused of racism has also affected white educators' practice around providing provide critical feedback across racial lines.

Although focused on undergraduate students rather than faculty educators, a 1998 study by Kent Harber[60] found that white students tend to supply more lenient feedback to a poorly written essay when they were led to believe via a photograph attached to the essay that the author was Black as opposed to essays assumed to be written by a white individual. Moreover, in 2012, Harber et al.[61] found a tendency for "positive bias" in public school teachers in which liberal white teachers excessively praised the work of their students of color. And in 2015, a study by Brenda Major, Jonathan Kunstman, Brenna Malta, Pamela Sawyer, Sarah Townsend, and Wendy Berry Mendes[62] found that students of color suspected that the positive feedback they received from white teachers were motivated more by their fear of appearing racist than objective criteria.

Research carried out by Alyssa Croft and Toni Schmader[63] further supports these findings. Their experiments focused on the motive for "feedback withholding bias," a phenomenon in which systemically marginalized students were denied critical feedback from white evaluators. Croft and Schmader conclude that their white informants avoided giving critical feedback not because of other-directed motives, that is, to protect the student, but rather because of self-interested motives stemming from fear of appearing prejudiced. Their experiments also found that individuals who were externally motivated and did not want to be perceived as prejudiced by others were more likely to withhold critical feedback than those who were internally motivated to be egalitarian.

When working with students of color, white educators may avoid critical feedback, offer no feedback, or overly praise students' work to avoid any suspicion of being racially prejudiced. Stephen Brookfield, who has already been mentioned because of his deep honesty and willingness to be vulnerable, acknowledges:

> In classes I catch myself holding back from challenging students of color and realize my so called "empathy" or desire to be an ally masks an embedded racist consciousness which says that "they" can't take a "strong" challenge from a White person. . . . Clearly, racism moves in me in small, micro-aggressive ways. I find myself quickly granting paper extensions to Black students and can only assume it springs from a White Supremacist judgment that because Black students are not as intelligent as White students, of course they will need more time to complete their work. I keep silent in a presentation given by a scholar of color because (so my internal calculus goes) my voice is so powerful it will diminish the voice of the presenter.[64]

Withholding critical feedback or lavishing praise on students' work, as Brookfield recognizes, may prove counterproductive and deny students the knowledge and skills they need to succeed. Moreover, it can communicate the message that little is expected from the student, reaffirming stereotypes that the educator might even intend to unsettle.

Sara Ahmed's critical discussion of "happy diversity talk"[65] suggests another dimension that helps us to understand why a white educator may avoid providing students of color with feedback. Ahmed's aim is to expose what happy talk obscures. She contends that the politics of feeling good even among those with commitments to social justice may mask the role of power and privilege, providing a way to avoid discomfort. Withholding feedback can be a way for white educators to maintain their comfort and to avoid conflict.

A study focused on the experiences of white professors who incorporate antiracist framework in the college classroom provides some additional insights. Jennifer Akamine Phillips, Nate Risdon, Matthew Lamsma, Angelica Hambrick, and Alexander Jun[66] found that white educators who see themselves as allies to students of color seek their affirmation and absolution. They refer to this as white individuals pursuing the "Black pat" which can, consequently, silence students of color who are compelled to show gratitude for white allyship. White allies' feelings, are again, recentered at the expense of students of color.

Students of color are often aware that they are not receiving the help they deserve. As one student of color protested about his white professors,

> I couldn't get any of my professors to give me critical feedback to tell me how to make my stuff better. Everything was oh, it's great, and I'm sitting here [thinking] I know there's something I can do. I know it can be better. Tell me how to make it better. . . . So for me it was like [I'm] not important enough for them to invest time and energy into making me better. [It's like] stop patting me on the head. . . . Stop patronizing me, you know.[67]

While many students of color want constructive critical feedback, they also want to be certain that the critical aspect of the feedback they are receiving is not derived from a negative stereotype. In *Whistling Vivaldi*, Claude Steele[68] explains:

> The mere fact of being black, in light of the stereotypes about it, creates a quandary over how to interpret critical feedback on academic work. Is the feedback based on the quality of their work or on negative stereotypes about their group's abilities? This ambiguity is often a contingency of black students' identity.[69]

In their research that expands the theory of stereotype threat, Geoffrey Cohen, Claude Steele, and Lee Ross[70] suggest ways of providing critical feedback across the racial divide in ways that ensure stereotypical messages are not conveyed.

Cohen et al. studied how critical feedback is received by the student when it is buffered by, first, an invocation of high standards and, second, is accompanied with an assurance of the student's capacity to meet those standards. When students of color received the "buffered" feedback, they attributed the critical nature of the feedback to rigorous standards rather than racial stereotypes. Cohen et al. introduce the term "the mentor's dilemma" which refers to the mentor's struggle to find ways to provide critical feedback without conveying a negative stereotypical message to the student. According to Cohen et al., educators who work across racial or gender lines must establish a learning context and a relationship with the student that will assure them that they are not being treated stereotypically.

The studies examining the mentor's dilemma and the solutions that follow from this research are embedded in and grow out of stereotype threat theory. Stereotype threat occurs when individuals are concerned about confirming a negative stereotype associated with the social group that they are a member of. The additional stress can negatively impact how they perform in certain academic situations. Claude Steele and Joshua Aronson[71] found that African American students demonstrate apprehension about confirming negative stereotypes around intelligibility and do not perform as well when they are reminded of the stereotype as when such reminders are absent. Based on their experiments, Steele and Aronson found that when race is made salient that Black college students underperformed on standardized tests and when race was not mentioned, the Black students performed more successfully. They concluded that the academic performance of marginalized students can be harmed by any implication that their performance might be viewed through the lens of negative stereotypes. The remedy for the mentor's dilemma, according to Cohen et al., is to ensure that stereotype threat is not triggered when the mentor gives critical feedback.

The topic of affirmation will be addressed subsequently. For now, it is important to note that the emphasis on stereotype threat in these studies addressing cross-racial feedback is narrow and limited, simplifying the challenge that giving critical feedback presents for the white educator, especially in the context of the white educator who is teaching critically about whiteness. Racial stereotype theory, given its psychological basis, tends to center what is in the individual's mind and overlooks the structural context within which stereotypes are embedded. Much like Fricker's focus on identity prejudice or implicit bias theory discussed in the previous chapter, stereotype threat theory, while emphasizing race, diverts attention from the structural and institutional dimension of racism and enables the core cause of racial injustice to remain uninterrogated. Consequently, deficit understandings of Black students' underperformance are reproduced, since it is the Black students' anxiety about stereotypes that is claimed to lead to underperformance.

Furthermore, as Daniel Craig McCloud[72] points out, racial stereotype threat theory is problematic because the reference to the "threat" of stereotypes assumes that African Americans need to be "reminded" about racism and stereotypes for academic performance to be impacted. McCloud underscores that for African Americans racism is very real and a constant presence, even when students are not given reminders. Explaining the underperformance of Black students by means of negative racial stereotypes implies that they are the ones who have a problem and draws attention away from the hegemonic structures of systemic white supremacy that negatively contribute to Black students' academic achievement as far back as elementary school. When the primary recommendation is that the educator buffer negative stereotype-triggers when they are giving feedback, then the larger structure of the systemic whiteness in schooling that impedes the flourishing of students of color can be underemphasized or, even, ignored.

In other words, racial stereotype threat theory does not take the whiteness of academia seriously and, thus, the mentor's dilemma might be more complex than Cohen et al. assume. The following three cases, both raising the issue of the whiteness of academia and white willful ignorance, demonstrate the drawbacks of relying on stereotype threat theory as a framework to understand the complicated role of white educators giving critical feedback to students of color.

In a discussion in a class whose topic was racism and education, a Black graduate student suggested that the concept of "epistemic oppression"[73] that is at the foundation of the historically white university should not be ignored. "*Epistemic* injustice?" the white professor exclaimed in dismissive tones. The student's self-doubt was immediately triggered, and she struggled to defend her use of the term and the way it links the ethical and epistemic dimensions of injustice. The student labored to explain how the concept points to the persistent epistemic exclusions that curtail one's ability to contribute to knowledge production. Nor did she name the theorist who introduced the term or the vast scholarship around it. The concept of epistemic oppression and the consequent harms to marginally situated knowers is exactly what the student was attempting to address, in the class discussion, and simultaneously experiencing.

Cases such as this, first, illustrate the limitations of appealing to stereotype threat to explain Black students' academic performance. It was not stereotype threat that triggered the Black student's performance but the tone of the question and the implied lack of credibility masquerading as scholarly inquiry on the part of the white educator. (Recall that Wekheiser argues that asking for reasons can be weaponized.) This understanding of what occurred with the Black student shifts attention away from a focus on deficit assumptions and draws attention to the willful ignorance of the white educator that the scholarship on epistemic injustice makes explicit. Second, the case underscores that although the white educator was not mistaken in her call for rigor (a student is reasonably expected to support the claims being made), white educators must be vigilant about their willful ignorance and the harmful effects of being suspicious of alternative epistemologies, and even what rigor might mean under alternative perspectives. The white educator's incredulity contributes to the maintenance of epistemic injustice which ironically was very likely what the student was attempting to address in her reference to epistemic oppression.

In her attempts to draw out the epistemic harms of microaggressions, Saba Fatima[74] offers additional cases that resonate with the situation previously described. In the first case, an academic researcher of color receives feedback on the manuscript that she submitted to a journal and the "comments are unusually harsh." Fatima illustrates the conflicting emotions that arose for this researcher. On the one hand, the researcher is made to feel "like an imposter who has nothing valuable to contribute to the field."[75] On the other hand, she recognizes that the comments reveal the reviewer's ignorance of the topic. Noting the condescending and sarcastic questions posed (for instance, in response to the term "white spaces," the reviewer asks, "Is this a country?"). Fatima exposes the microaggressive dimensions of this question and its epistemic harms.

In another case, Fatima relates that at a job interview, a scholar of color was asked, "Do you think your research fits within educational research?"[76] While dominantly situated knowers might perceive this as a benign inquiry, a request to locate the candidate's scholarship in the field of education, Fatima demonstrates that the question does not ask *how* the candidate's scholarship fits but *whether* it fits, insinuating that it does not fit. The scholar of color is made to feel like "an alien to the discipline."[77] Moreover, when the candidate replies to this question by saying that her scholarship not only fits, but if it does not, that it should, her reply remains unintelligible to the interviewers. The candidate relates that she was not expecting this question, especially posed in this way, exclusionary and admonishing, implying that a person of color is "incapable of being rational and intellectual enough"[78] for academia. The possible erosion of self-trust, the reinforcing of stereotypes, and the protection of willful ignorance helps explain how academia remains white especially when a question is not only an inquiry but is weaponized.

Cultivating a vigilant vulnerably informed humility can support white educators' attempts to better understand when offering critical feedback to students of color is a form of epistemic violence. A vigilant vulnerably informed humility does not insist that rigor be abandoned and does not abjure giving critical feedback. Rather, such humility can draw attention to *how* feedback is given and when it is framed through the lens of white willful ignorance. While a white person telling a person of color that they are not correctly interpreting the oppression that they daily experience is problematic and a dismissive tone only further upholds epistemic injustice, this does not imply that educators should refrain from critical feedback when appropriate. In the same vein, vigilant vulnerably informed humility cautions white educators to be aware when they are whitesplaining or reframing the experience of people of color to fit dominant frameworks of intelligibility. Being vigilant about the limits of one's understanding of oppression is a feature of such humility. Nevertheless, humility does not require the uncritical acceptance of everything students of color say or do. Uncertainty and openness, especially about systems of dominance, counter a not needing to know and a resistance to knowing, as described in previous chapters.

Thus, the humility being called for involves a humility against the certainty and the exclusive closure of dominant epistemological frameworks that authorize and encourage dominantly situated knowers to immediately doubt and dismiss what marginally situated knowers say and in ways that are camouflaged by good intentions. As Leonardo and Porter advise us regarding the recounting of marginalized experience, one should not focus "on their individual accuracy but on their collective experiences and the perspectives born from a life of risk."[79]

Fostering vigilant vulnerably informed humility underscores that giving constructive critical feedback necessitates being careful to recognize when to avoid contributing to epistemic injustice. Dominant epistemologies often define and limit what is valued as scholarship in academia and who is entitled to produce knowledge. The barriers that marginally situated knowers encounter when they attempt to reshape dominant epistemologies are insidious and frustrating, as the scholarship in the previous chapters bears out. In her attempts to describe university diversity workers, Ahmed refers to the metaphor of "institutional plumber."[80] University diversity workers, she explains, attempt to unblock the system when the blockage upholds how the system works. In other words, the systems function by obstructing those who are trying to transform it. The institution prevents the real blockage from being removed in ways that do not seem that this is what is being done. Understanding that students of color are often trying to transform a system that uses "reasonableness" and "logic" often draped with good intentions as armor can offer white educators some guidance in how they give critical feedback.

When feedback continuously perpetuates epistemic injustice, students of color may consequently decide to withdraw from the path to the professoriate questioning whether it is a worthwhile goal to pursue. Consequently, valuable knowledges that encourage the production of counter-narratives challenging systemic white supremacy in academia may be lost.

Vigilant vulnerable humility suggests that when white educators consider giving students of color, critical feedback they must seriously reflect: What are the standards upon which critical feedback is based that might support and protect white willful ignorance and diminish the experiences of our students of color? Epistemic humility and the openness of vulnerability require that truth and sound evidence not be considered as fixed and conclusive, and it encourages a willingness to stay in the discomfort that might reveal how deeply whiteness affects subjectivity and what the subject ostensibly knows.

Moreover, since complicity in structures of power and privilege must vigilantly be at the forefront, white educators who offer feedback to their students of color must consider the discursive effects of their good intentions. Even when emanating from humility, the interdependent and relational understanding of subjectivity must be appreciated so that moral goodness, white solipsism, or white saviorism is not restored.

Vigilance, vulnerability, and humility demand a profound frankness about how white educators engage with students of color. Chinnery advances vulnerability as openness "to that which might shatter our knowledge, our identities, and even our self-understanding as knowing subjects."[81] Educators, as Dozono and Taylor contend, must not resist considering their complicity in "legacies of epistemic injustice." Vigilant vulnerable informed humility appeals to the decentering of dominantly situated knowledge, dominantly situated ways of interpreting the social world, and opens a space for attending to the needs and interests of the marginalized as they navigate a system that ultimately devalues their epistemological framework and does not take the quality of their education seriously.

In their study of the racialized experience of Black students, Jessica Harris and Chris Linder[82] offer a quote from an interview with a Black graduate student who explains:

> I come (into the classroom) with views knowing the historical background of America with African Americans and how slavery went about and the injustices in our educational systems. When I put those views out, people like to either be defensive or argumentative, thinking that I'm wrong. I'm like, "No, I'm not wrong." But because they don't have to necessarily go through it or they don't necessarily see it, they don't get it.[83]

Harris and Linder emphasize that white faculty educators must work to honor and validate the experience of students of color given the dismissiveness they negotiate every day. When white educators give feedback, they must continually educate themselves about patterns of incredulity that students of color experience. This does not mean refusing to give feedback but instead to develop ways to disrupt the default skepticism students of color encounter and taking care not to contribute to it. Affirmation is key for white educators who give constructive critical feedback to students, as the research around the mentor's dilemma correctly intimates. A closer investigation, however, shows that affirmation is complex and does not necessarily mean the same thing as only giving praise.

In 2008, Mary Rowe,[84] whose work focuses on organizational development and who studies mentoring and recruitment practices, introduced the concept micro-affirmations to counter what is now commonly referred to as microaggressions. Rowe defined micro-affirmations as "apparently small acts, which are often ephemeral and hard-to-see, events that are public and private, often unconscious but very effective, which occur wherever people want to help others succeed."[85] The concept micro-affirmations helped her develop methods for supervisors to effectively mentor and support their mentees from underrepresented communities. Rolón-Dow and Davison[86] explain that micro-affirmations are more than just acts of kindness. They define micro-affirmations as

> behaviors, verbal remarks or environmental cues experienced by individuals from minoritized racial groups in the course of their everyday lives that affirm

their racial identities, acknowledge their racialized realities, resist racism or advance cultural and ideological norms of racial justice.[87]

In their attempts to demonstrate that micro-affirmations are more than just acts of kindness, they propose three types of micro-affirmations: microcompliments, microsupport, and microvalidations. Microcompliments are subtle communications that convey a message that one's identity or heritage is appreciated. Microsupports are small verbal or nonverbal actions that affirm a sense of belonging. Microvalidation are small but subtle ways that a student's thoughts, abilities, or feelings are affirmed.

While other typologies of micro-affirmations have been advanced, the significant point to highlight is that micro-affirmations aim to disrupt social injustice and marginalization. In their study of mentoring for first-generation college students, James Ellis, Candice Power, Cynthia Demetriou, Carmen Huerta-Bapat, and A. T. Panter[88] recommend that faculty and staff

> recognize the effects of microaggressions as they appear within students and their own reflections. A critical skill that distinguishes micro-affirmations from surface-level kindness is using a deep understanding of systems of power and privilege to determine which words, what tone, and which experience to use to address students' affected self-concept in college.[89]

This call for affirmation does not reject the possibility of giving critical feedback, but rather points to the need for vigilance around the giving of feedback so that it contributes to dismantling rather than reifying epistemic injustice.

Another way of describing affirmation is intimated in what Pohlhaus[90] refers to as "echoing" and it is especially significant because echoing itself can serve as an oppositional response to epistemic injustice. Pohlhaus introduces the term "echoing" to refer to the epistemic resistance that often is dismissed by dominantly situated knowers as "unreasonable." She demonstrates how echoing is a collective response to oppression and entails epistemic labor. Drawing attention away from the one-on-one encounters that the scholarship around gaslighting sometimes emphasizes, Pohlhaus develops a concept of structural epistemic gaslighting to describe the structural context and the conditions that gaslight nondominantly situated knowers when they are, in fact, doing collective-resistant labor. She defines structural epistemic gaslighting as when a person, practice, image, or institution exerts unwarranted pressure on epistemic agents to doubt their own perceptions.[91]

Echoing is a response to structural epistemic gaslighting. Pohlhaus' reference to good echoing that can be affirmational can play a role in white educators' interactions with students of color. According to Pohlhaus:

Finding and maintaining sources of good echoing can be critical when one is subject to systematic and structural forms of epistemic gaslighting. This sort of *good echoing* can help one to maintain warranted self-trust and stability of beliefs in the face of unwarranted epistemic pressures to doubt them.[92]

As Pohlhaus maintains, however, echoing is not only about affirmation.

Pohlhaus examines two types of echoing that are a response to epistemic gaslighting: survival echoing and resistant echoing. Survival echoing is a positive and general way to name the type of resistance necessary for survival because "being intelligible to oneself is a necessary component of epistemic life."[93] It may manifest in withdrawing or disengaging from conversations even when such withdrawal is criticized as "counterproductive" because it shuts down the conversation. Pohlhaus contends that such accusations are a form of gaslighting because, in fact, what is being shut down by the critique is resistance to epistemic oppression. When disengagement is not recognized as a form of resistance and is mischaracterized as refusing to engage, this mischaracterization is a form of shutting down perspectives that resist recentering dominant frameworks of intelligibility. Pohlhaus argues that far being a way of shutting down conversations or disengaging from difficult thinking, *such echoing can be a demand for a different conversation.*

Pohlhaus also describes a second form of echoing, resistant echoing, that is discernable when one repeats a point when it seems it is not taken as seriously as it should be. The important point is that resistant echoing is not just about repeating marginalized belief. It is about affirmation but also more than that. The power of echoing is also noted in Jose Medina[94] concept of echoing used to explain how individual acts of resistance get echoed or repeated by others until a sea change occurs and new attitudes, beliefs, and patterns of behavior become part of the common framework of intelligibility. Pohlhaus insists that when enough resistant knowers reverberate marginalized hermeneutical concepts in the context of epistemic gaslighting, it becomes possible to counter gaslighting and open space for new meanings in the collective epistemic framework. As she puts it, "When (marginalized beliefs and claims) reverberate loud enough, they can begin to dismantle the features of our practices, institutions, and selves that support epistemic gaslighting."[95]

Thus, resistant echoing is not just "irrational group think," but, rather, it is a form of resistance to recentering dominant frameworks and the epistemic gaslighting that contributes to maintaining such recentering. When uptake is denied a marginalized belief, concept, or interpretation, echoing can be a resistant response that is itself a form of uptake.

Pohlhaus's insistence on the value of good echoing requires emphasizing three points. First, epistemic gaslighting is not necessarily about creating a psychological breakdown but instead an epistemic breakdown. Epistemic gaslighting is structural because it is oriented toward putting out of circulation "a particular way of understanding the world, one that centers the experience of the one who is gaslit."[96] Next, responses to epistemic gaslighting are not only about affirmation but also about resistance. As Alison Bailey underscores in her introduction to the journal volume in which Pohlhaus' argument is published:

> Resistant knowers need a significant amount of echoing to sustain their beliefs. They also need resistant communities of knowers to affirm and stabilize those beliefs.[97]

Echoing not only reflects a form of solidarity but also represents a form of active resistance that opposes the pressures that suppress marginally situated knowers' beliefs from circulating. When marginalized frameworks are ignored, echoing can make possible reverberations that are collectively loud enough that the conditions that support epistemic gaslighting can be unsettled.

Finally, Pohlhaus also draws attention to identity as intersectional, one can be both dominant in one aspect of one's identity and nondominant in another. She cautions that those who are engaged in echoing consider:

> To whom and with whom am I making sense?
> For whom are our interactions providing room for making sense and for whom are they not?
> Where are the silences in these ways of making sense and what might those silences tell us?[98]
> Underscoring how echoing can hurt other marginalized groups, Pohlhaus offers the example of the use of ableist metaphors that are echoed in epistemologies of ignorance. She advocates addition questions to consider when engaging in resistant echoing:
> How is the sense of these experiences able to travel and circulate?
> How and why are my claims being afforded reception?[99]

Echoing (no pun intended) the call for vigilance underscored in many of the chapters of this book, Pohlhaus cautions that "these questions need to be revisited again and again, since claims that once echoed resistantly can be coopted in ways that disintegrate their resistant sense."[100]

At this point, it should be clear that echoing is a richly complicated form of affirmation that can combat the white willful ignorance that Black students often encounter in the classroom and in their campus culture. Counter to what John McWhorter[101] argues when he decries the oversensitivity of Black college students who he maintains subscribe to a cult of victimology that leads them to embrace anti-intellectualism and mistakes minor inconveniences for racism, echoing is not a form of coddling. On the other hand, echoing is also not a form of saviorism. To affirm students of color in the way that leads to white saviorism is again to center whiteness. Instead, echoing is an acknowledgment of the willful ignorance that generates the violence, not only psychological and physical but also epistemic, that Black students endure.

Echoing is a type of affirmation that white educators can implement to counter the microaggressions that students of color experience in the classroom and on campus. Some additional questions white educators might reflect upon:

In what ways can I help my students acquire the skills and knowledge they need in ways that puts them (rather than me) at the center of their learning? How am I teaching and assessing my students in ways that value white ways of thinking while devaluing their own knowledge and skills?

The point that follows from this discussion of epistemic gaslighting and the role of echoing is that feedback must always be given in a way that reduces epistemic oppression and does not contribute to it.

CONCLUSION

This chapter attempts to apply some of the scholarship discussed in previous chapters to three challenges that white educators often encounter when they teach about whiteness to racially diverse students. It aims to raise the issue of how white educators can negotiate their complicity in structures of racial injustice while simultaneously recognizing that they cannot transcend such complicity so long as unjust structures persist. The first challenge critically examines a common pedagogical assumption, teach students where they are at. The second challenge relates to an ambiguity the white educator might experience around white students' learning and the violence it generates in the classroom. Finally, the third challenge analyzes the question of cross-racial critical feedback from the lens of vigilant vulnerably informed humility. Rather than a list of what white educators must do or not do, guiding questions to consider are posed. That there are not checklists is underscored by the emphasis on vigilance and the need to stay in the discomfort of uncertainty so that new possibilities are given credibility. That said, I hope that more research will be undertaken to more clearly understand how the type of humility advocated here concretely facilitates the pursuit of knowledge because such humility makes it easier for alternative ideas to be taken seriously.

Leonardo and Porter caution whites not to turn "racism into an intellectualist problem, rather than a lived one."[102] It must be clear that as a white educator who teaches about whiteness to a racially diverse group of students, these challenges are very personal to me. It took me a while to recognize that it is not sufficient to just include more works by scholars of color into my curriculum and to realize that how I teach is just as important as what I teach. The point of this chapter, and indeed this book, is the hope that these arguments will serve as an invitation and as provocation for further dialogue and critique. Ongoing collaboration with colleagues, researchers, and students can reduce the sidelining of the racial realities of students of color. Such collaboration can encourage the creation of rich educational opportunities where students of color can engage in learning that explicitly demonstrates that their lives and lived experiences matter.

NOTES

1. Carol Schick, "By Virtue of Being White: Resistance in Anti-racist Pedagogy." *Race, Ethnicity, and Education* 3, no. 1 (2010): 83–101.

2. Ibid., 97.

3. Sara Ahmed, "Declarations of Whiteness: The Non-Performativity of Anti-Racism," *Borderlands e-journal* 3, no. 2 (2004), http://www.borderlandsejournal.adelaide.edu.au/vol3no2_2004/ahmed_declarations.htm

4. Kate Manne, *Down Girl: The Logic of Misogyny* (New York: Oxford University Press, 2018): xxi. In her analysis of the concept of misogyny, Manne note the catch 22 in such an examination and cautions that examining the phenomenon one is liable to reproduce it.

5. Ann Chinnery, "Revisiting 'The Master's Tools': Challenging Common Sense in Cross-Cultural Teacher Education." *Equity & Excellence in Education* 4, no. 4 (2008): 395–404.

6. Ibid., 395.

7. George Yancy, "Dear White America." *The New York Times* (December 24, 2015).

8. Robin DiAngelo and Ozlem Sensoy, "Getting Slammed: White Depictions of Race Discussions as Arenas of Violence." *Race, Ethnicity, and Education* 17, no. 1 (2014): 103–128.

9. Ibid. 105.

10. Carina Maye, "I Really Wanted this to Be a Poem." Dept. of Art & Art Education, Teachers College cited in Teaching While White (Columbia Medical School) Powerpoints & PDF's — Stephen D. Brookfield (stephenbrookfield.com) (2020),

11. Zeus Leonardo and Ronald Porter, "Pedagogy of Fear: Toward a Fanonian Theory of "Safety" in Race Dialogue." *Race, Ethnicity and Education* 13, no. 2 (2010):139–157.

12. Ibid., 149.

13. Ibid., 139.

14. Ann Chinnery, "Revisiting 'the Master's Tools.'"

15. Ibid., 395.

16. Cheryl Matias, "On the 'Flip' Side: A Teacher Educator of Color Unveiling the Dangerous Minds of White Teacher Candidates." *Teacher Education Quarterly* 40, no. 2 (2013): 53–73.

17. Ibid., 54.

18. Ibid.

19. Mark Chesler & Alford A. Young Jr., "Faculty Members' Social Identities and Classroom Authority." *New Directions for Teaching and Learning* 111 (2007): 11–19.

20. Edith Samuel & Njoki Wane, "'Unsettling Relations': Racism and Sexism Experienced by Faculty of Color in a Predominantly White Canadian University." *Journal of Negro Education* 74, no. 1 (2005): 76–87.

21. Derald Wing Sue, G. C. Torino, C.M. Capodilupo, D.P. Rivera, & Lin, A. I., "How White Faculty Perceive and React to Difficult Dialogues on Race: Implications for Education and Training." *The Counseling Psychologist* 37 (2009): 1090–1115; Laura Smith, Susan Kashubeck-West, Gregory Payton, and Eve Adams, "White Professors Teaching About Racism: Challenges and Rewards" *The Counseling Psychologist* 45, no. 5 (2017): 651–668.

22. Stephen Brookfield, "Uncovering and Challenging White Supremacy." In George Yancy, ed., *Education for Critical Consciousness* (New York: Routledge, 2019): 11–27.

23. Ibid., 13.

24. Stephen Brookfield, "The Dynamics of Teaching about Race." In his edited volume, *Teaching Race: How to Help Students Unmask and Challenge Racism* (New York: Wiley, 2018): 1–18.

25. Ibid., 8.

26. Stephen Brookfield, "Critical Thinking and Its Limitations: Can We Think Our Way Out of White Supremacy?" In Elizabeth Minnich and Michael Quinn Patton, eds, *Thought Work: Thinking, Action, and the Fate of the World* (Lanham, MD: Rowman & Littlefield, 2019): 154.

27. Robin DiAngelo, "White Fragility." *International Journal of Critical Pedagogy* 3, no. 3 (2011): 54.

28. I focus on Brookfield's work because not only does he address the challenges of teaching while white, he does so with incredible honesty and vulnerability. As he puts it in his PowerPoints: "What does it mean for white instructors to teach in a multiracial classroom in a way that takes account of the racial identities everyone brings to the table?" Teaching While White (Columbia Medical School) PowerPoints & PDF's—Stephen D. Brookfield (stephenbrookfield.com).

29. Ann Curry-Stevens, "New Forms of Transformative Education: Pedagogy for the Privileged." *Journal of Transformative Education* 5 no. 1 (2007): 33–58.

30. Ibid., 45.

31. Zeus Leonardo, "The Colour of Supremacy: Beyond the Discourse of 'White privilege'." *Educational Philosophy and Theory* 36 no. 2 (2004): 137–152.

32. Ibid. 137.
33. Ann Curry-Stevens, "New Forms of Transformative Education," 49.
34. Zeus Leonardo, "The Colour of Supremacy," 141.
35. Deanna Blackwell, "Sidelines and Separate Spaces: Making Education Anti-Racist for Students of Color." *Race, Ethnicity, and Education* 13, no. 4 (2010): 473–494).
36. Ibid., 474.
37. Ibid., 485.
38. William A. Smith, Tara J. Yosso, Daniel G. Solórzano, "Challenging Racial Battle Fatigue on Historically White Campuses: A Critical Race Examination of Race-Related Stress." In Christine Stanley, ed., *Faculty of Color: Teaching in Predominately White Colleges and Universities* (Bolton, MA: Anker Publishing, 2006): 299–327.
39. Alison Jones, "The Limits of Cross-Cultural Dialogue: Pedagogy, Desire, and Absolution in the Classroom." *Educational Theory* 49, no. 3 (1999): 299–316.
40. Ibid., 302.
41. Zeus Leonardo & Ronald Porter, "Pedagogy of Fear," 140.
42. Kristie Dotson, "Accumulating Epistemic Power: A Problem with Epistemology." *Philosophical Topics* 46, no .1 (2018): 129–154.
43. Kristie Dotson, "Tracking Epistemic Violence, Tracking Practices of Silencing," *Hypatia* 26, no. 2 (2011): 236–257.
44. Alison Jones, "The Limits of Cross-Cultural Dialogue," 308.
45. https://www.nytimes.com/2019/05/18/opinion/sunday/doug-glanville-cubs.html
46. Kathy Hytten and John Warren, "Engaging Whiteness: How Racial Power Gets Reified in Education," *Qualitative Studies in Education* 16, no. 1 (2003): 65–89.
47. Ibid., 79.
48. Derald Wing Sue, *Microaggressions in Everyday Life: Race, Gender, and Sexual Orientation* (New York: Wiley and Sons, 2010): xvi.
49. George Yancy, *Black Bodies, White Gazes: The Continuing Significance of Race* (Lanham, MD: Rowman and Littlefield, 2008).
50. Karen Tao, Jesse Owen and Joanan Drinane, "Was *that* Racist? An Experimental Study of Microaggression Ambiguity and Emotional Reactions for Racial–Ethnic Minority and White Individuals." *Race and Social Problems* 9, no.4 (2017): 262–271.
51. Saba Fatima, "On the Edge of Knowing: Microaggressions and Epistemic Uncertainty as a Woman of Color." In Kirsti Cole and Holly Hassel, eds., *Surviving Sexism in Academia: Feminist Strategies for Leadership* (New York: Routledge 2017): 147–154.
52. Ibid. 148.
53. Sara Ahmed, "Declarations of Whiteness: The Non-Performativity of Anti-Racism." *borderlands* e-journal 3, no. 2 (2004). http://www.borderlands.net.au/vol3no2_2004/ahmed_declarations.htm
54. Ibid.
55. Ibid.

56. Elizabeth Spelman, "Managing Ignorance." In Shannon Sullivan and Nancy Tuana, eds., *Race and Epistemologies of Ignorance* (Albany, NY: State University of New York Press, 2007): 119–131.

57. Marilyn Frye, *The Politics of Reality: Essays in Feminist Theory* (Trumansburg, NY: The Crossing Press, 1983).

58. Alexis Shotwell, *Knowing Otherwise: Race, Gender, and Implicit Understanding* (University Park, PA: Pennsylvania State University, 2011).

59. John McWhorter, "The Dehumanizing Condescension of White Fragility." The Atlantic, July 15, 2020 How 'White Fragility' Talks Down to Black People - The Atlantic.

60. Kent Harber, "Feedback to Minorities: Evidence of a Positive Bias." *Journal of Personality and Social Psychology* 74, no. 3 (1998): 622–628.

61. Kent D. Harber, Jamie L. Gorman, Frank P. Gengaro, Samantha Butisingh, William Tsang, Rebecca Ouellette, "Students' Race and Teachers' Social Support Affect the Positive Feedback Bias in Public Schools." *Journal of Educational Psychology* 104, no. 4 (2012): 1149–1161.

62. Brenda Major, Jonathan Kunstman, Brenna Malta, Pamela Sawyer, Sarah Townsend and Wendy Berry Mendes, "Suspicion of Motives Predicts Minorities' Responses to Positive Feedback in Interracial Interactions." *Journal of Experimental Social Psychology* 62 (2015): 75–88.

63. Alyssa Croft and Toni Schmader, "The Feedback Withholding Bias: Minority Studies Do Not Receive Critical Feedback from Evaluators Concerned about Appearing Racist." *Journal of Experimental Social Psychology* 48 (2012): 1139–1144.

64. Stephen Brookfield, "Chapter 6: Using Narrative and Team-Teaching to Address Teaching about Racial Dynamics." In, C. Scott & J. Sims, eds., *Developing Workforce Diversity Programs, Curriculum and Degrees in Higher Education* (Hershey, PA: IGI Publishing, 2016): 98–116, 104.

65. Sara Ahmed, *On Being Included: Racism and Diversity in Institutional Life* (Durham, NC: Duke University Press, 2011).

66. Jennifer Akamine Phillips, Nate Risdon, Matthew Lamsma, Angelica Hambrick and Alexander Jun, "Barriers and Strategies by White Faculty Who Incorporate Anti-Racist Pedagogy." *Race and Pedagogy Journal: Teaching and Learning for Justice* 3, no. 2 (2019): 2–19.

67. Melanie Acosta, Shaunte Duggins, Thomas Moore, Thomasenia Adams, and Bridgette Johnson, "'From Whence Cometh My Help?' Exploring Black Doctoral Student Persistence." *Journal of Critical Scholarship on Higher Education and Student Affairs* 2, no. 1 (2015): 32–48, 40.

68. Claude Steele, *Whistling Vivaldi: How Stereotypes Affect Us and What We Can Do* (New York: W. W. Norton & Company, 2010).

69. Ibid., 162.

70. Geoffrey Cohen, Claude Steele, and Lee Ross, "The 'Mentor's Dilemma': Providing Critical Feedback Across the Racial Divide." *Personality and Social Psychology Bulletin* 25, no. 10 (1999): 1302–1318.

71. Claude Steele and Joshua Aronson, "Stereotype Threat and the Intellectual Test Performance of African-Americans." *Journal of Personality and Social Psychology* 69, 5 (1995): 797–811.

72. Daniel Craig McCloud, *Racial Stereotype Threat: A Critical Perspective.* Thesis and Dissertation, 525 (2016). https://ir.library.illinoisstate.edu/etd/525.

73. Kristie Dotson, "Conceptualizing Epistemic Oppression." *Social Epistemology* 28, no. 2 (2014): 115–138.

74. Saba Fatima, "'I Know What Happened to Me: The Epistemic Harms of Microaggressions." In J.W. Schroer and L. Freeman, eds., *Microaggressions and Philosophy* (New York: Routledge, 2020): 163–183.

75. Ibid., 172.

76. Ibid., 173.

77. Ibid.

78. Ibid.

79. Zeus Leonardo & Ronald Porter, "Pedagogy of Fear," 154.

80. https://feministkilljoys.com/2017/10/24/institutional-as-usual/

81. Ibid.

82. Jessica Harris and Chris Linder, "The Racialized Experiences of Students of Color in Higher Education and Student Affairs Graduate Preparation Programs." *Journal of College Student Development* 59, no. 2 (2018): 141–158.

83. Ibid., 150.

84. Mary Rowe, "Micro-affirmation and Micro-inequalities." *Journal of the International Ombudsman Association* 1, no. 1 (2008): 1–9.

85. Ibid., 4.

86. Rosalie Rolón-Dow and A. Davison, "Racial Microaffirmations: Learning from Student Stories of Moments that Matter." In J. M. Jones, ed., *Diversity Discourse: Research Briefs from the Center for the Study of Diversity*, Vol. 1(4) (Newark, DE: University of Delaware, 2018): 1–9.

87. Ibid., 1.

88. James Ellis, Candice Powel, Cynthia Demetriou, Carmen Huerta-Bapat, and A.T. Panter, "Examining First-Generation College Student Lived Experiences with Microaggressions and Microaffirmations at a Predominantly White Public Research University." *Cultural Diversity and Ethnic Minority Psychology* 25, no. 2 (2019): 266–279.

89. Ibid., 11.

90. Gaile Pohlhaus Jr., "Gaslighting and Echoing, or Why Collective Epistemic Resistance is not a 'Witch Hunt.'" *Hypatia* 35, no. 4 (2020): 674–686.

91. Ibid., 679.

92. Gaile Pohlaus Jr., 682.

93. Ibid., 682.

94. Jose Medina, *The Epistemology of Resistance: Gender and Racial Oppression, Epistemic Injustice, and Resistant Imaginations* (New York: Oxford University Press, 2013): 233.

95. Ibid., 683.

96. Ibid., 677.

97. Alison Bailey, "On Gaslighting and Epistemic Injustice: Editor's Introduction." *Hypatia* 35, no. 4 (2020): 671.

98. Gaile Pohlhaus Jr. 684.

99. Ibid.

100. Ibid.

101. Guest host John McWhorter on college campus safe spaces (slate.com) and Antiracism, Our Flawed New Religion (thedailybeast.com).

102. Zeus Leonardo & Ronald Porter, "Pedagogy of Fear," 149.

Chapter 5

Cultivating a Vigilantly Vulnerable Informed Humility

Scholarship studying white educators that teach courses around antiracism and systemic white supremacy either focus on how white educators navigate *their own discomfort* teaching the material (uncertainty, guilt, defensiveness) or the challenges they encounter teaching the material *to white students* (white students' resistance to discomfort).[1] Laura Smith and her colleagues[2] studied white professors who struggle with multicultural impostor syndrome, multicultural perfectionism, and multicultural projections. As an illustration of the challenges that white educators encounter, one of the white researchers relates a personal story of her own conflicting feelings about her pedagogy.

The white researcher/educator recounts how she gave the inordinate amount of attention to a group of white female students who both verbally and nonverbally were resisting the idea that racism still exists. These students also continually denied that they were privileged by their whiteness. The white researcher/educator offers an important but partial insight in describing her struggle:

> I recognized that the heightened attention I gave them might come at the expense of other students who were really engaging with the material, and/or those students who experience racism. In other words, I began to wonder if perhaps I was privileging these already privileged students in ways that I might not want to. I thought about how all the worrying that I did about these students might not even improve their chances of changing. Does my increased attention help them lower their resistance to the material? How much was I shortchanging the other students in class?[3]

The white researcher/educator continues to explain that one of these students was eventually moved by the educator's efforts and, at the end of the term, the student expressed how she has grown from the course. Although the white researcher/educator mentions the other students in the class, she does not explain how they were impacted. More explicitly, what did students of color have to sacrifice for these white female students' learning?

Jennifer Akamine Phillips et al.[4] similarly address the barriers that white educators encounter when they teach about racism and whiteness. They highlight the lack of institutional commitment, the hazards they experienced with tenure and promotion, and their internalized struggles with white identity (i.e., *the educators'* white identity). One white participant recounted how she felt disappointed because of the lack of recognition from Black faculty for the antiracist and allyship work that she does. Phillips et al. refer to this as white educators needing a "Black pat" of affirmation. Another white participant noted that she did not know how to connect with her Black students, and she acknowledged that it was something she "needed to put extra effort into . . . in order for a certain level of trust to be established."[5] Some of the strategies that Phillips et al. recommend is that white educators must recognize their white privilege, their white complicity, and avoid performing allyship.

The arguments in this book are intended to expand upon this research by emphasizing the dangers of recentering white student resistance and white educators' feelings and needs. This is not to invalidate the need for studying challenges that white educators encounter but, instead, to inquire if focusing exclusively on white educators' challenges can be consistent with attempts to *decenter* white peoples' needs, desires, and emotions so that the needs, desires, and emotions of students of color are not sideline and students of color are not harmed. I acknowledge that even writing a book about white educators such as this risks recentering whiteness yet again.

While designing a class that teaches about whiteness, it is not only necessary to include the works of scholars of color on the syllabus. The work of some scholars of color, important as the insight they provide are, may still address a white audience. There is a vast body of scholarship around whiteness by scholars of color, however, that center the needs and interests of students of color. The scholarship reviewed in these chapters has underscored how important it is for white educators to examine their pedagogy and consider how whiteness is recentered when the educator mistakenly assumes that what white students need is what all students need. Moreover, the research discussed in the chapters puts emphasis on combating willful ignorance as a prerequisite for white educators who want to better understand how to encourage the flourishing of students of color in predominantly white institutions. The call for white teachers to cultivate a vigilantly vulnerable informed humility that can help white educators examine their own practices offers a way to help make students of color matter in courses that teach about whiteness.

Cultivating a vigilantly vulnerable informed humility requires a decentering of white desires, feelings, and needs and necessitates a willingness to avoid defending white innocence and sheltering willful ignorance. Such humility entails letting go of the need for approval from one's white students who can be appeased by protecting their comfort or of the need for absolution from one's students of color. Such humility involves being willing to rock the boat.

In *Living a Feminist Life*, Sara Ahmed[6] personally reflects upon and theorizes her own journey of becoming a feminist and how feminism is a way of "making sense of what doesn't make sense."[7] Ahmed offers a phenomenology of the development of a feminist consciousness as "a sensible reaction to the injustices of the world."[8] A central figure in this book is the feminist killjoy, a trope that Ahmed first explored in her earlier book *The Promise of Happiness*,[9] in which she critiques the ideal of happiness that women are persuaded to strive for. Those who interrupt this happiness narrative are pejoratively labeled "killjoys" because it is claimed that they kill others' joy. They are accused by those who uphold the pillars of patriarchy as being bitter and unhappy. Such conventional notions of happiness compel women to conform to femininity and "give up having a will of one's own."[10]

This happiness myth, according to Ahmed, requires one to trade in one's own desires, one's own beliefs *to keep the peace and make others happy*. While I have been arguing that white educators must decenter their own needs, this pressure to make others happy can negatively affect white female educators, too. In an inspiring discussion, Ahmed explains that capitulating to such notions of happiness is also a way of "avoiding what one cannot bear"[11] because those who may not be able to orient to the demands of femininity become "affect aliens"[12] (those who feel at odds with the world or feel that the world is odd). This parallels many of the arguments made in previous chapters about how systemic white supremacy is maintained and how willful ignorance is shielded from critique. White educators may avoid challenging white students or may be unwilling to be a killjoy of her white students' happiness. But Ahmed passionately insists,

> I am not willing to make happiness my cause. . . . Not making happiness your cause can cause unhappiness. A killjoy is willing to cause unhappiness.[13]

A feminist killjoy is willing to make people uncomfortable, challenging them to critically reflect on their investments in happiness. Put differently, a feminist killjoy is willing to acknowledge *how models of happiness may depend on the oppression of others*. White educators might seriously consider how their happiness and their comfort depend on the oppression of students of color in their classrooms. Ahmed contends that to be a feminist is to be willing to make trouble. As Ahmed explains, "To become feminist is to kill other people's joy, to get in the way of other people's investments."[14] She describes the killjoy as someone who is willing to point out injustices even at the risk of being blamed for being the problem rather than people blaming the injustice that the killjoy exposes.

Ahmed offers a provocative insight that white educators would do well to remember. According to Ahmed, although the feminist killjoy is seen by some as the one who *causes* bad feelings, she is merely *exposing* the bad feeling that already exists but is concealed. A story about Ahmed's family dinner table illustrates this point. In voicing her disagreement with a racist remark made by someone in her family, Ahmed notices that the happy mood recedes and the atmosphere is drenched in the silence of bad feelings. Yet Ahmed realizes that it is not the killjoy who caused the bad feeling but instead it was the family member who made the racist remark that brought negativity into the room. Feminists are often attributed as the origin of bad feelings, as the ones who ruin the atmosphere *as if by exposing the problem one becomes the problem*. A white educator might bear in mind that the ostensible happiness of her white students is linked to the unhappiness of her students of color. When a white educator becomes a feminist killjoy, she is not causing bad feelings but, rather, exposing the bad feeling that already exists in the class but is concealed.

It is true that by speaking up as a killjoy, one risks the loss of belonging, the loss of being "with." The consequences of rocking the boat can mean that you must risk sacrificing the loss of a warm relationship with white students who respond with white fragility to counter any of their own discomforts. Still, Ahmed reclaims the negative label of killjoy, turning it into a positive aspiration. As she puts it, "to kill joy is to open a life, to make room for life, to make room for possibility, for chance,"[15] and for alternative ways of living, or for new pedagogical approaches.

Ahmed explicitly clarifies that being a killjoy means being willing to kill not only others' joy but also *one's own*. "Sometimes being a feminist killjoy," she writes, "can feel like you are getting in the way of your own happiness."[16] It is important to consider whether such happiness depends upon ignoring the injustices that we are implicated in. To borrow a phrase from a later article by Ahmed,[17] white educators must be willing to "rock the boat." Ahmed's work is inspirational and counterbalances anyone who may assume that vigilantly vulnerable informed humility entails passivity. Instead, she underscores that such humility can help one to recognize when speaking up is appropriate while at the same time acknowledging when silence is called for.

For the white educator teaching about whiteness to a diverse group of students, learning to be an educator killjoy is to be willing to cause unhappiness and to be willing to live with the consequences of what she is willing. At a related but pressing level, it is to be willing to question what one believes it means to be a good educator and to interrogate the joy of teaching that we seek, but that may be preventing us from noticing the injustices we partake in. First and foremost, to become a killjoy is to be willing to question the types of pedagogical successes and pleasures that one strives for when one teaches and when these aspirations for happiness might block what needs to be considered when "good" teaching contributes to harm of others. What does the joy in teaching to which we aspire make comfortable? What does it make difficult to notice? Ahmed exhorts us to always remember that our happiness might depend on what we do not notice.

An additional insight glean from Ahmed's work on the feminist killjoy is that white educators must live with what we wish to transform. Ahmed's work can remind white educators to remain vigilantly attentive to the disorientation necessary for disrupting willful ignorance.

As a white woman who has been taught to tolerate things I disagree with as a strategy for being loved and as a method of survival, I have been taught to shun "rocking the boat." But this comes at a cost of allowing me to ignore discomforting conflict at a moment when I should not look away. I need to become better at recognizing and disrupting whiteness, even when that means taking risks, so that students of color do not have to and so that students of color do not have to endure unchallenged violence in the classroom.

How does one develop a sensitivity to distinguish between silence and speech? I turn to Linda Martin Alcoff's call for white double consciousness as an attempt to draw the outlines of the *type of sensitivity* that opposes and attempts to reduce willful ignorance.

Linda Martin Alcoff's[18] recent work on white double consciousness complements the call to be willing to rock the boat that is key to cultivating vigilantly vulnerable informed humility. Borrowing from Du Bois's concept of Black double consciousness, Alcoff advocates that white people cultivate white double consciousness. Alcoff contrasts these two types of double consciousness. Black double consciousness describes the psychic situation of oppressed groups who to survive racism need to see themselves through two sets of perspectives, their own perspective as well as their oppressors. For Alcoff, white double consciousness involves white people coming to see themselves not only through the dominant white lens but to be willing to see themselves as they are perceived from nondominant perspectives. As Alcoff puts it, white people can experience double consciousness when they begin to understand themselves "through both the dominant and non-dominant lens and *recognising the latter as a critical corrective truth.*"[19]

Significant for the white double consciousness that Alcoff invokes is that it entails white people realizing that the knowledge and lens of the systemically oppressed is a crucial corrective truth. Alcoff clarifies that, unlike the white gaze that oppresses Blacks, the split consciousness between the way white people comprehend themselves and the way that they are perceived by marginalized groups is not oppressive to white people. Moreover, while for Black double consciousness, it is the inner lens that is a more reliable indicator of truth than the external one, for white double consciousness, the internal lens is unreliable because it is exclusively dependent on dominant frameworks.[20] Only by being open to the external perspective can this unreliability be fractured.

For instance, bell hooks[21] explains that in the Black imagination whiteness is represented as "a terrorizing imposition, a power that wounds, hurts, tortures," something difficult for white people to acknowledge because it would "disrupt the fantasy of whiteness as representing goodness."[22] On Alcoff's account of white double consciousness, the uncomfortable tension generated by taking seriously how whiteness is perceived in the Black imagination can be a valuable tool for the type of disorientation that opens a space for activism that is more about supporting others than gleaning rewards for oneself. Antiracism work that is guided by a white lens, Didi Delgado reminds us, is inherently flawed.[23] Cultivating a critical white double consciousness can guide the white educator to be more attuned to inhabiting the critique and to knowing when, where, and how to rock the boat. Critical white double consciousness can contribute to actively combating willful ignorance and cultivating vigilantly vulnerable informed humility.

Being willing to combat white willful ignorance is key to developing white racial consciousness. Dana Francisco Miranda[24] offers a clarifying extension and re-shifting of Alcoff's interpretation of DuBois's double consciousness based on the contemporary works of Paget Henry and Jane Anna Gordon. Double consciousness, Miranda explains following Henry, develops in two ways potentiated and un-potentiated because recognizing two perspectives, and especially the external view that offers the ability to see oneself through the eyes of the white other, does not guarantee that one will acquire a critical perspective on that external view. As Miranda puts it, seeing oneself through the eyes of the white other can also lead to "duplicity, resentment and resignation." Potentiated double consciousness, in contrast, offers a critical capability that "gives the Africana subject special subjective access and insight into the dehumanizing caricature of the African."[25]

Double consciousness as a possibility for white people, Miranda, citing Gordon,[26] explains, functions differently than it does for Black people. Living the oppressive conditions of the white world inherently creates contradiction and tension that can lead to criticality. For white people, however, white consciousness is systemically supported and firmly intact, inherently dependent on the rejection of the Black gaze. Whereas the pain of oppression can motivate Black people toward a potentiated double consciousness, split consciousness for white people is only possible if white people are willing to avoid protecting white innocence and willful ignorance. The arguments in this book have attempted to underscore the significance of combating desires for white innocence that are protected by and protect willful ignorance. Cultivating vigilantly vulnerable humility moves in this direction but as the emphasis on "vigilance" demands, a potentiated white double consciousness is a continual struggle, as long as systemic white supremacy persists.

Alcoff's notion of white double consciousness works hand in hand with Ahmed's notion of being willing to rock the boat because the experience of disorientation that the latter produces can facilitate the cultivation of white double consciousness. At the same time, white double consciousness can encourage a willingness to rock the boat. Because double consciousness invokes the idea of seeing oneself through conflicting meaning systems, it can be uncomfortably disorientating but at the same time open up both critique of self and the broader structures within which one is embedded. Being willing to risk the discomfort of rocking the boat and being willing to stay in that discomfort can help white educators better understand when their pedagogy is oppressive to students of color, as well as when what is considered as challenges to pedagogy serve as opportunities for disavowal or escape. Holding multiple consciousnesses in tension, as Medina proposes, can not only ground critical reflexivity but also establish richer understandings of the effects of one's pedagogy on systemically racially marginalized students.

I recognize that these arguments remain highly theoretical. I hesitate to provide any how-to-do solutions to the complex pedagogical concerns raised in this chapter. There are no concrete strategies and no checklists because vigilance is always necessary. Checklists will never be a cure to the problem of systemic white supremacy in education, and they can often reproduce systemic injustice when they become just that, a check in a box that allows one to assume one has done good. Throughout this book, it has been underscored how good white intentions can have harmful consequences for students of color. The aim of the book was to apply theoretical insights that can help the white educator to better recognize the effects of their good intentions so that they can disrupt the ensuing harms. Moreover, acknowledging the dangers of white researchers turning whiteness "into an intellectualist problem, rather than a lived one,"[27] I hope the arguments in this book do not remain at the theoretical level and, instead, serve to invite further dialogue and critique around these concerns. I hope that the critical theoretical insights that have been explored in this book can contribute to the possibility of white educators becoming more aware of how to teach to the needs of all students.

NOTES

1. Elizabeth Denevi and Nick Pastan, "Helping Whites Develop Anti-Racist Identities: Overcoming their Resistance to Fighting Racism." *Multicultural Education* 14, no. 2 (2006): 70–73; Elizabeth Denevi, "White-on-White: Exploring White Racial Identity, Privilege, and Racism." *Independent School* 63, no. 4 (2004): 78–87.

2. Laura Smith, Susan Kashubeck-West, Gregory Payton, and Eve Adams, "White Professors Teaching about Racism: Challenges and Rewards." *The Counseling Psychologist* 45, no. 5 (2017): 651–668.

3. Ibid., 660.

4. Jennifer Akamine Phillips, Nate Risdon, Matthew Lamsma, Angelica Hambrick and Alexander Jun, "Barriers and Strategies by White Faculty who Incorporate Anti-Racist Pedagogy." *Race & Pedagogy Journal* 3, no. 2 (2019): 1–27.

5. Ibid., 10.

6. Sara Ahmed, *Living a Feminist Life* (Durham, NC: Duke University Press, 2017): 257–258.

7. Ibid., 21.

8. Ibid.

9. Sara Ahmed, *The Promise of Happiness* (Durham, NC: Duke University Press, 2010).

10. Ibid., 62.

11. Ibid., 64.

12. Ibid., 42.

13. Sara Ahmed, *Living a Feminist Life* (Durham, NC: Duke University Press, 2017): 257–258.

14. Sara Ahmed, *Living a Feminist Life*, 65

15. Sara Ahmed, *The Promise of Happiness*, 20.

16. Ibid.

17. Sara Ahmed, "Rocking the Boat: Women of Colour as Diversity Workers." In Jason Arday and Heidi Safia Mirza, eds., *Dismantling Race in Higher Education: Racism, Whiteness and Decolonsing the Academy* (New York: Palgrave, 2018): 331–348.

18. Linda Martin Alcoff, *The Future of Whiteness* (Malden, MA: Polity Press, 2015).

19. Ibid. 140. Emphasis mine.

20. See Zeus Leonardo, "Whiteness Studies and Educational Supremacy: The Unbearable Whiteness of Schooling," in his *Race Frameworks: A Multidimensional Theory of Racism and Education* (New York: Teachers College Press, 2013): 96.

21. bell hooks, "Representing Whiteness in the Black Imagination." In her *Black Looks: Race and Representation* (London: Turnaround, 1992).

22. Ibid., 169.

23. DiDi Delgado, "Whites Only: SURJ And The Caucasian Invasion of Racial Justice Spaces." https://www.huffpost.com/entry/whites-only-surj-and-the-caucasian-invasion-of-racial_b_58dd5cf7e4b04ba4a5e25209

24. Dana Francisco Miranda, *Signals Crossed: White Double Consciousness and the Role of the Critic* (Urbana, IL: Philosophy of Education Society, in press).

25. Paget Henry, "Gender and Africana Phenomenology," *The C.L.R. James Journal* 17, no. 1 (2011): 157.

26. Jane Anna Gordon, "Legitimacy from Modernity's Underside: Potentiated Double Consciousness." *Worlds & Knowledges Otherwise* 1, no. 3 (2006): 1–21.

27. Zeus Leonardo and Ronald Porter, "Pedagogy of Fear: Toward a Fanonian Theory of "Safety" in Race Dialogue." *Race, Ethnicity and Education* 13, no. 2 (2010): 149.

Bibliography

Acosta, Melanie, Shaunte Duggins, Thomas Moore, Thomasenia Adams, and Bridgette Johnson. "'From Whence Cometh My Help?' Exploring Black Doctoral Student Persistence." *Journal of Critical Scholarship on Higher Education and Student Affairs* 2, no. 1 (2015): 32–48, 40.

Afxentiou, Afxentis, Robin Dunford and Michael Neu, eds. *Exploring Complicity: Concept, Cases and Critique* (New York: Rowman & Littlefield, 2017).

Afxentiou, Afxentis, Robin Dunford and Michael Neu. "Introducing Complicity." In their edited collection *Exploring Complicity: Concept, Cases and Critique* (New York and London: Rowman & Littlefield International, 2017): 1–17.

Ahmed, Sara. "Declarations of Whiteness: The Non-Performativity of Anti- Racism." *borderlands* 3, no. 2 (2004). http://www.borderlandsjournal.adelaide.edu.au/vol3no2_2004/ahmed_declarations.htm.

Ahmed, Sara. *On Being Included: Racism and Diversity in Institutional Life* (Durham, NC: Duke University Press, 2012).

Ahmed, Sara. "Rocking the Boat: Women of Colour as Diversity Workers." In *Dismantling Race in Higher Education: Racism, Whiteness and Decolonsing the Academy*, eds. Jason Arday and Heidi Safia Mirza (New York: Palgrave, 2018): 331–348.

Ahmed, Sara. "The Phenomenology of Whiteness." *Feminist Theory* 8, no. 2 (2007): 149–168.

Ahmed, Sara. *The Promise of Happiness* (Durham: Duke University Press, 2010).

Alcoff, Linda Martin. "Epistemic Identities." *Episteme* 7, no. 2 (2010): 128–137.

Alcoff, Linda Martin. *The Future of Whiteness* (Malden, MA: Polity Press, 2015): 168–170.

Alcoff, Linda Martin and Elizabeth Potter, eds., *Feminist Epistemologies* (New York: Routledge, 1993).

Alfano, Mark, Michael Lynch and Alessandra Tanesini. *The Routledge Handbook of Philosophy of Humility* (New York: Routledge, 2021).

Ansely, Frances Lee. "Stirring the Ashes: Race, Class and the Future of Civil Rights Scholarship." *Cornell Law Review* 74, no. 6 (1989): 993–1077.

Applebaum, Barbara. *Being White, Being Good: White Complicity, White Moral Responsibility, and Social Justice Pedagogy* (Lanham, MD: Lexington Books, 2020).

Baehr, Jason. *The Inquiring Mind: On Intellectual Virtues and Virtue Epistemology* (Oxford: Oxford University Press, 2011).

Bailey, Alison. "On Gaslighting and Epistemic Injustice: Editor's Introduction." *Hypatia* 35, no. 4 (2020): 671.

Bailey, Alison. "On White Shame and Vulnerability." *South African Journal of Philosophy* 30, no. 4 (2011): 472–483.

Bailey, Alison. *The Weight of Whiteness: A Feminist Engagement with Privilege, Race, and Ignorance* (Lanham, MD: Lexington Books, 2021).

Bailey, Alison. "'White Talk' as a Barrier to Understanding Whiteness." In *White Self-Criticality beyond Anti-racism: How Does It Feel to Be a White Problem?*, ed. George Yancy (Lanham, MD: Lexington Books, 2014): 37–57.

Baldwin, James. "As Much Truth as One Can Bear." *The New York Times* (January 14, 1962).

Baldwin, James. *The Price of the Ticket: Collected Nonfiction 1948–1985* (New York: St. Martin's Press, 1985).

Battaly, Heather. "Can Humility be a Liberatory Virtue?" In *The Routledge Handbook of Philosophy of Humility* (New York: Routledge, 2021): 170–184.

Berenstain, Nora. "Epistemic Exploitation." *Ergo* 3, no. 22 (2016): 569–590.

Berlak, Ann. "Teaching and Testimony: Witnessing and Bearing Witness to Racisms in Culturally Diverse Classrooms." *Curriculum Inquiry* 29, no. 1 (1999): 99–127.

Bialystok, Lauren. "How Open Should Open-Mindedness Be?" *Educational Theory* 69, no. 4 (2019): 534.

Bialystok, Lauren and Matt Ferkany. "Open-mindedness from the Public Sphere to the Classroom." *Educational Theory* 69, no. 4 (2019): 377–381.

Blackwell, Deanna. "Sidelines and Separate Spaces: Making Education Anti-Racist for Students of Color," *Race, Ethnicity, and Education* 13, no. 4 (2010): 473–94.

Bonilla-Silva, Eduardo. *Racism without Racists: Color-Blind Racism and the Persistence of Racial Inequality in America* (New York: Rowman & Littlefield, 2017).

Bowman, Melanie. "Privileged Ignorance, 'World'-Traveling, and Epistemic Tourism." *Hypatia* 35 (2020): 475–489.

Bridges, Christopher, and Peter Mather. "Joining the Struggle: White Men as Social Justice Allies." *Journal of College and Character* 16, no. 3 (2015): 155–168, 162.

Brookfield, Stephen. "Chapter 6: Using Narrative and Team-Teaching to Address Teaching about Racial Dynamics." In *Developing Workforce Diversity Programs, Curriculum and Degrees in Higher Education*, eds. C. Scott and J. Sims (Hershey, PA: IGI Publishing, 2016): 98–116, 104.

Brookfield, Stephen. "Killing White Innocence: A Review of George Yancy's *Backlash: What Happens When We Talk Honestly About Race.*" *Tikkun* (April 23, 2018) Killing White Innocence | Tikkun.

Brookfield, Stephen. "The Dynamics of Teaching about Race." In his edited volume, *Teaching Race: How to Help Students Unmask and Challenge Racism* (New York: Wiley, 2018): 1–18.

Brookfield, Stephen. "Uncovering and Challenging White Supremacy." In *Education for Critical Consciousness*, ed. George Yancy (New York: Routledge, 2019): 11–27.

Brookfield, Stephen. "White Teachers in Diverse Classrooms: Using Narrative to Address Teaching About Racial Dynamics." In *Developing Workforce Diversity Programs, Curriculum and Degrees in Higher Education*, eds. C. Scott and J. Sims (Hershey, PA: IGI Publishing, 2016): 98–117.

Butler, Judith. "Explanation and Exoneration, or What We Can Hear." *Social Text* 72, 20, no. 3 (2002): 177–188.

Butler, Judith. *Precarious Life: The Powers of Mourning and Violence* (New York: Verso, 2004).

Case, Kim and Annette Hemmings, "Distancing: White Women Preservice Teachers and Antiracist Curriculum," *Urban Education* 40, no. 6 (2005): 606–626.

Chavez Chavez, Rudolfo and James O'Donnell, *Speaking the Unpleasant: The Politics of (non)Engagement in the Multicultural Education Terrain* (Albany, NY: State University Press, 1998).

Chesler, Mark and Alford A. Young, Jr., "Faculty Members' Social Identities and Classroom Authority." *New Directions for Teaching and Learning*, 111 (2007): 11–19.

Chinnery, Ann. "On Epistemic Vulnerability and Open-mindedness." In *Philosophy of Education 2013*, ed. Cris Mayo (Urbana, IL: Philosophy of Education Society, 2013): 63–66.

Chinnery, Ann. "Revisiting 'The Master's Tools': Challenging Common Sense in Cross-Cultural Teacher Education." *Equity & Excellence in Education* 4, no. 4 (2008): 395–404.

Chizhik, Estella Williams and Alexander Williams Chizhik. "Are you Privileged or Oppressed? Students' Conceptions of Themselves and Others" *Urban Education* 40, no. 2 (2005): 116–143.

Code, Lorraine. *Rhetorical Spaces: Essays on Gendered Locations* (London: Routledge, 1995).

Cohen, Geoffrey, Claude Steele, and Lee Ross. "The 'Mentor's Dilemma': Providing Critical Feedback Across the Racial Divide." *Personality and Social Psychology Bulletin* 25, no. 10 (1999): 1302–1318.

Collins, Patricia Hill. *Black Feminist Thought: Knowledge, Consciousness, and the Politics of Empowerment* (London: Routledge, 1990).

Croft, Alyssa and Toni Schmader, "The Feedback Withholding Bias: Minority Studies Do Not Receive Critical Feedback from Evaluators Concerned about Appearing Racist." *Journal of Experimental Social Psychology* 48 (2012): 1139–1144.

Curry-Stevens, Ann. "New Forms of Transformative Education: Pedagogy for the Privileged." *Journal of Transformative Education* 5 no. 1 (2007): 33–58.

Daniels, Julia and Heather Hebard. "Complicity, Responsibility, and Authorization: A Praxis of Critical Questioning for White Literacy Educators." *English Teaching: Practice and Critique* 17, no. 1 (2018): 16–27.

Davidson, Lacey."When Testimony Isn't Enough: Implicit Bias Research as Epistemic Exclusion." In *Overcoming Epistemic Injustice: Social and Psychological Perspective*, eds. Benjamin Sherman and Stacey Goguen (Lanham, MD: Rowman & Littlefield, 2019): 269–283.

Daum, Courtenay. "White Complicity." *New Political Science*, 42, no. 3 (2020): 443–449.

de Castillo, Lori Gallegos "Review of José Medina's *The Epistemology of Resistance: Gender and Racial Oppression, Epistemic Injustice, and Resistant Imaginations*." *APA Newsletter on Hispanics in Philosophy* 13, no. 2 (Spring 2014): 15–17.

DiAngelo, Robin. "White Fragility." *International Journal of Critical Pedagogy* 3, no. 3 (2011): 54–70.

DiAngelo, Robin. *White Fragility: Why It's So Hard for White People to Talk about Racism* (Boston, MA: Beacon Press, 2018).

DiAngelo, Robin and Ozlem Sensoy. "Getting Slammed: White Depictions of Race Discussions as Arenas of Violence." *Race, Ethnicity, and Education* 17, no. 1 (2014): 103–128.

Dotson, Kristie. "A Cautionary Tale: On Limiting Epistemic Oppression." *Frontiers: A Journal of Women Studies* 33, no. 1 (2012): 24–47.

Dotson, Kristie. "Accumulating Epistemic Power: A Problem with Epistemology." *Philosophical Topics* 46, no .1 (2018): 129–154.

Dotson, Kristie. "Conceptualizing Epistemic Oppression." *Social Epistemology* 28, no. 2 (2014): 115–138.

Dotson, Kristie. "Tracking Epistemic Violence, Tracking Practices of Silencing." *Hypatia* 26, no. 2 (2011): 236–257.

Dozono, Tadashi and Rebecca Taylor. "Teaching for Open-mindedness: A Justice-Oriented Approach." *Educational Theory* 69, no. 4 (2019): 473–490.

Driver, Julia. "Modesty and Ignorance." *Ethics* 109, no. 4 (1999): 827–834.

Driver, Julia. "The Virtues of Ignorance." *Journal of Philosophy* 86, no. 7 (1989): 373–384.

Driver, Julia. *Uneasy Virtue* (New York: Cambridge University Press, 2001).

Du Bois, W. E. B. *The Souls of Black Folk* (Boston: Bedford Books, 1920).

Eddo-Lodge, Reni. *Why I'm No Longer Talking to White People About Race* (New York: Bloomsbury, 2017).

Ellis, James, Candice Powel, Cynthia Demetriou, Carmen Huerta-Bapat, and A. T. Panter. "Examining First-Generation College Student Lived Experiences with Microaggressions and Microaffirmations at a Predominantly White Public Research University." *Cultural Diversity and Ethnic Minority Psychology* 25, no. 2 (2019): 266–279.

Ellison, Ralph Waldo. *Invisible Man* (New York: Vintage, 1995).

Fatima, Saba. "'I Know What Happened to Me: The Epistemic Harms of Microaggressions." In *Microaggressions and Philosophy*, eds. J. W. Schroer and L. Freeman (New York: Routledge, 2020): 163–183.

Fatima, Saba. "On the Edge of Knowing: Microaggressions and Epistemic Uncertainty as a Woman of Color." In *Surviving Sexism in Academia: Feminist Strategies for Leadership*, eds. Kirsti Cole and Holly Hassel (New York: Routledge 2017): 147–154.

Fellows, Mary Louise and Sherene Razack. "The Race to Innocence: Confronting Hierarchical Relations Among Women." *Journal of Gender, Race and Justice* 1 (1998): 335–352.

Foste, Zak. "Remaining Vigilant: Reflexive Considerations for White Researchers Studying Whiteness." *Whiteness and Education* 5, no. 3 (2020): 1–16.

Foucault, Michel. *The History of Sexuality Vol. 2* (New York: Vintage Books, 1985).

Foucault, Michel. "The Subject and Power." *Critical Inquiry* 8, no. 4 (1982): 777–795.

Frankenberg, Ruth. "The Mirage of Unmarked Whiteness." In *The Making and Unmaking of Whiteness*, eds. Birgit Brander Rasmussen et al. (Durham, NC: Duke University Press, 2001): 72–96.

Frankenberg, Ruth. *White Women, Race Matters: The Social Construction of Whiteness* (Minneapolis, MN: University of Minnesota Press, 1993).

Fricker, Miranda. *Epistemic Injustice: Power and the Ethics of Knowing* (Oxford: Oxford University Press, 2007).

Fricker, Miranda. "Epistemic Justice as a Condition of Political Freedom." *Synthese* 190 (2013): 1317–1332.

Fricker, Miranda. "Evolving Concepts of Epistemic Injustice." In *The Routledge Handbook of Epistemic Injustice*, eds. J. Kidd, J. Medina, and G. Pohlhaus (New York: Routledge, 2017): 53–60.

Fricker, Miranda. "Replies to Alcoff, Goldberg, and Hookway on *Epistemic Injustice*." *Episteme* 7, no. 2 (2010): 164–178.

Friedlaender, Christina. "On Microaggressions: Cumulative Harm and Individual Responsibility." *Hypatia* 22, no. 1 (2018): 5–21.

Frye, Marilyn. *The Politics of Reality: Essays in Feminist Theory* (New York: Crossing Press, 1983).

Frye, Marilyn. *Willful Virgin: Essays in Feminism 1976–1992* (Freedom, CA: Crossing Press).

Gillborn, David. "Rethinking White Supremacy: Who Counts in 'WhiteWorld'?" *Ethnicities* 6, no. 3 (2006): 318–240.

Gilson, Erinn. *The Ethics of Vulnerability: A Feminist Analysis of Social Life and Practice* (New York: Routledge, 2013).

Gilson, Erinn. "Vulnerability, Ignorance, and Oppression." *Hypatia* 26, no. 2 (2011): 308–332.

Greco, John. "Intellectual Humility and Contemporary Epistemology: A Critique of Epistemic Individualism, Evidentialism and Internalism." In *The Routledge Handbook of Philosophy of Humility* (New York: Routledge, 2021): 271–282.

Hamad, Ruby. *White Tears/Brown Scars: How White Feminism Betrays Women of Color* (New York: Catapult, 2020).

Harber, Kent. "Feedback to Minorities: Evidence of a Positive Bias." *Journal of Personality and Social Psychology* 74, no. 3 (1998): 622–628.

Harber, Kent, Jamie Gorman, Frank Gengaro, Samantha Butisingh, William Tsang, and Rebecca Ouellette. "Students' Race and Teachers' Social Support Affect the Positive Feedback Bias in Public Schools." *Journal of Educational Psychology* 104, no. 4 (2012): 1149–1161.

Hare, William. *In Defense of Open-mindedness* (Montreal, QC: McGill-Queen's University Press, 1985).

Hare, William. *Open-mindedness and Education* (Montreal, QC: McGill-Queen's University Press, 1979).

Hare, William. "The Ideal of Open-Mindedness and Its Place in Education." *Journal of Thought* 38, no. 2 (2003): 3–10.

Harris, Cheryl. "Whiteness as Property," *Harvard Law Review* 106, no. 8 (1993): 1707–1791.

Harris, Jessica and Chris Linder. "The Racialized Experiences of Students of Color in Higher Education and Student Affairs Graduate Preparation Programs." *Journal of College Student Development* 59, no. 2 (2018): 141–158.

Harvin, Cassandra Byers. "Conversations I Can't Have." *On the Issues* 5, no. 2 (1996): 15–16.

hooks, bell. *Ain't I a Woman: Black Women and Feminism* (2nd edition) (New York: Routledge, 2015).

hooks, bell. *Black Looks: Race and Representation* (Boston, MA: South End Press, 1992).

Houston, Barbara. "A Conversation Beyond Argument: On a Bridge Over Troubled Waters." *Philosophy of Education Society 1997* (Urbana-Champaign, IL: University of Illinois, 1998): 25–29.

Hughes, Langston. *The Ways of White Folk* (New York: A.A. Knopf, 1969).

Hunt II, Cecil. "The Color of Perspective: Affirmative Action and the Constitutional Rhetoric of White Innocence." *Michigan Journal of Race and Law* 11 (2006): 477–555.

Hytten, Kathy and John Warren, "Engaging Whiteness: How Racial Power Gets Reified in Education." *Qualitative Studies in Education* 16, no. 1 (2003): 65–89.

Jones, Alison. "The Limits of Cross-Cultural Dialogue: Pedagogy, Desire, and Absolution in the Classroom." *Educational Theory* 49, no. 3 (1999): 299–316.

Jonsson, Terese. *Innocent Subjects: Feminism and Whiteness* (Pluto Press, 2021).

Kidd, I. J., "Intellectual Humility, Confidence, and Argumentation." *Topois*, 35 (2016): 395–402.

Kutz, Christopher. *Complicity: Ethics and Law for a Collective Age* (Cambridge: Cambridge University Press, 2000).

Kwong, Jack. "Open-mindedness as Engagement." *Southern Journal of Philosophy* 54, no. 1 (2016): 70–86.

Langton, Rae. "Review: Epistemic Injustice: Power and the Ethics of Knowing." *Hypatia* 25, no. 2 (2010): 459–464.

Lee, Harper. *To Kill a Mockingbird* (Philadelphia, PA: Lippincott, 1960).

Leonardo, Zeus. "The Colour of Supremacy: Beyond the Discourse of 'White privilege'." *Educational Philosophy and Theory* 36 no. 2 (2004): 137–152.

Leonardo, Zeus. "The Myth of White Ignorance." In his *Race, Whiteness and Education* (New York: Routledge, 2009): 107–125.

Leonardo, Zeus and Ronald Porter. "Pedagogy of Fear: Toward a Fanonian Theory of "Safety" in Race Dialogue." *Race, Ethnicity and Education* 13, no. 2 (2010): 139–157.

Lorde, Audre. *Sister Outsider: Essays and Speeches* (Berkeley, CA: Crossing Press, 1984).

Lugones, Maria. *Pilgrimages Peregrinajes: Theorizing Coalition Against Multiple Oppressions* (Lanham, MD: Rowman & Littlefield, 2003).

Lugones, Maria and Elizabeth Spelman. "Have We Got a Theory for You! Feminist Theory, Cultural Imperialism and the Demand for 'the Woman's Voice.'" *Women's Studies International Forum* 6, no. 6 (1983): 573–581.

Major, Brenda, Jonathan Kunstman, Brenna Malta, Pamela Sawyer, Sarah Townsend and Wendy Berry Mendes, "Suspicion of Motives Predicts Minorities' Responses to Positive Feedback in Interracial Interactions." *Journal of Experimental Social Psychology* 62 (2015): 75–88.

Manne, Kate. *Down Girl: The Logic of Misogyny* (New York: Oxford University Press, 2018).

Mason, Rebecca. "Two Kinds of Unknowing." *Hypatia* 26, no. 2 (2011): 294–307.

Matias, Cheryl. "On the 'Flip' Side: A Teacher Educator of Color Unveiling the Dangerous Minds of White Teacher Candidates." *Teacher Education Quarterly* 40, no. 2 (2013): 53–73.

Maye, Carina. "I Really Wanted this to Be a Poem." Dept. of Art & Art Education, Teachers College cited in *Teaching While White* (Columbia Medical School) Powerpoints & PDF's — Stephen D. Brookfield (stephenbrookfield.com) (2020).

Mayo, Cris. "Vertigo at the Heart of Whiteness." In *Philosophy of Education 2000*, ed. Lynda Stone (Urbana, IL: Philosophy of Education Society, 2001): 317–320.

McCloud, Daniel Craig. *Racial Stereotype Threat: A Critical Perspective*. Thesis and Dissertation, 525 (2016). https://ir.library.illinoisstate.edu/etd/525.

McIntyre, Alice. *Making Meaning of Whiteness: Exploring Racial Identity with White Teachers* (Albany, NY: State University of New York Press, 1997).

McWhorter, John. "The Dehumanizing Condescension of White Fragility." *The Atlantic*, July 15, 2020.

Medina, Jose. "Hermeneutical Injustice and Polyphonic Contextualism: Social Silences and Shared Hermeneutical Responsibilities." *Social Epistemology* 26, no. 2 (2012): 201–220.

Medina, Jose. "On Refusing to Believe: Insensitivity and Self-Ignorance." In José María Ariso and Astrid Wagner, eds., *Rationality Reconsidered: Ortega y Gasset and Wittgenstein on Knowledge, Belief, and Practice* (Berlin: De Gruyter, 2016): 187–200.

Medina, Jose. "Response to Beth Sperry, Chris Lowry, and Gaile Pohlhaus." *Social Philosophy Today* 30 (2014): 207–216.

Medina, Jose. *The Epistemology of Resistance: Gender and Racial Oppression, Epistemic Injustice, and Resistant Imaginations* (New York: Oxford University Press, 2013).

Mills, Charles. *Blackness Visible: Essays on Philosophy and Race* (Ithaca, NY: Cornell University Press, 1998).

Mills, Charles. *The Racial Contract* (Ithaca, NY: Cornell University Press, 1997).

Mills, Charles. "White Ignorance." In *Race and Epistemologies of Ignorance*, eds. Shannon Sullivan and Nancy Tuana (Albany, NY: State University of New York Press, 2007): 13–38.

Mills, Charles. "White Supremacy as Sociopolitical System: A Philosophical Perspective." In *White Out: The Continuing Significance of Racism*, eds. Ashley "Woody" Doane and Eduardo Bonilla-Silva (New York: Routledge, 2003): 35–48.

Monteverde, Giuliana. "Navigating Complicity in Contemporary Feminist Discourse." In *Exploring Complicity: Concept, Cases and Critique*, eds. Afxentis Afxentiou, Robin Dunford and Michael Neu (New York: Rowman & Littlefield, 2017): 99–118.

Morrison, Toni. *Playing in the Dark: Whiteness and the Literary Imagination* (New York: Vintage Books, 1992).

Moreton-Robinson, Aileen. *Talkin' Up to the White Woman: Indigenous Women and Feminism* (Queensland: University of Queensland Press, 2000).

Orozco, Richard and Jesus Jaime Diaz. "'Suited to their Needs': White Innocence as a Vestige of Segregation." *Multicultural Perspectives* 18, no. 3 (2016): 127–133.

Ortega, Mariana. "Being Lovingly, Knowingly Ignorant: White Feminism and Women of Color." *Hypatia* 21, no. 3 (2006): 56–74.

Phillips, Jennifer Akamine, Nate Risdon, Matthew Lamsma, Angelica Hambrick and Alexander Jun, "Barriers and Strategies by White Faculty Who Incorporate Anti-Racist Pedagogy." *Race and Pedagogy Journal: Teaching and Learning for Justice* 3, no. 2 (2019): 2–19.

Pohlhaus, Jr., Gaile. "Discerning the Primary Epistemic Harm in Cases of Testimonial Injustice," *Social Epistemology* 28, no. 2 (2014): 99–114.

Pohlhaus, Jr., Gaile. "Gaslighting and Echoing, or Why Collective Epistemic Resistance is not a 'Witch Hunt.'" *Hypatia* 35, no. 4 (2020): 674–686.

Pohlhaus, Jr., Gaile. "Relational Knowing and Epistemic Injustice: Toward a Theory of Willful Hermeneutical Ignorance." *Hypatia* 27, no. 4 (2012): 715–735.

Pohlhaus, Jr., Gaile. "Resistance and Epistemology: A Response to Jose Medina's *The Epistemology of Resistance*." *Social Philosophy Today* 30 (2014): 187–195.

Probyn, Fiona. "Playing Chicken at the Intersection: The White Critic in/of Critical Whiteness Studies." *Borderlands* 13, no. 2 (2004). http://www.borderlandsejournal.adelaide.edu.au/vol3no2_2004/probyn_playing.htm

Probyn-Rapsey, Fiona. "Complicity, Critique, and Methodology." *Ariel* 38, no. 2–3 (2007): 65–82.

Richardson, Troy. "Open-mindedness in a 'Post-Truth' Era." *Educational Theory* 69, no. 4 (2019): 439–453.

Riggs, Wayne. "Open-mindedness." *Metaphilosophy* 41, nos. 1–2 (2010): 172–188.

Robinson, Brian. "'I am So Humble!': On the Paradoxes of Humility." In *The Routledge Handbook of Philosophy of Humility* (New York: Routledge, 2021): 26–35.

Roediger, David, ed. *Black Writers on What It Means to Be White* (New York: Schocken Books, 1998).

Roediger, David. *The Wages of Whiteness: Race and the Making of the American Working Class* (New York and London: Verso. 1991).

Rolón-Dow, Rosalie, and A. Davison. "Racial Microaffirmations: Learning from Student Stories of Moments that Matter." In *Diversity Discourse: Research Briefs from the Center for the Study of Diversity*, ed. J. M. Jones, Vol. 1(4) (Newark, DE: University of Delaware, 2018): 1–9.

Roman, Leslie. "Denying (White) Racial Privilege: Redemption Discourses and the Use of Fantasy." In *Off White: Readings on Race, Power and Society*, ed. M. Fine (New York: Routledge, 1997): 270–282.

Roman, Leslie. "White is a Color! White Defensiveness, Postmodernism and Anti-racist Pedagogy." In *Race, Identity and Representation in Education*, ed. Cameron McCarthy and Warren Crinchlow (New York: Routledge, 1993): 71–88.

Ross, Thomas. "The Rhetorical Tapestry of Race: White Innocence and Black Abstraction." *William & Mary Law Review* 32, no. 1 (1990): 1–40.

Rowe, Mary. "Micro-affirmation and Micro-inequalities." *Journal of the International Ombudsman Association* 1, no. 1 (2008): 1–9.

Samuel, Edith and Njoki Wane. "'Unsettling Relations': Racism and Sexism Experienced by Faculty of Color in a Predominantly White Canadian University." *Journal of Negro Education* 74, no. 1 (2005): 76–87.

Sanders, Mark. *Complicities: The Intellectual and Apartheid* (Indiana: Duke University Press, 2002).

Schick, Carol. "By Virtue of Being White: Resistance in Anti-Racist Pedagogy." *Race, Ethnicity, and Education* 3, no. 1 (2010): 83–101.

Shotwell, Alexis. *Knowing Otherwise: Race, Gender, and Implicit Understanding* (University Park, PA: Pennsylvania State University, 2011).

Smith, Laura, Susan Kashubeck-West, Gregory Payton, and Eve Adams. "White Professors Teaching About Racism: Challenges and Rewards" *The Counseling Psychologist* 45, no. 5 (2017): 651–668.

Smith, William. "Higher Education: Racial Battle Fatigue." In *Encyclopedia of Race, Ethnicity, and Society*, ed. R. T. Schaefer (Thousand Oaks, CA: Sage, 2008): 615–618.

Smith, William, Tara Yosso, and David Solorzano. "Challenging Racial Battle Fatigue on Historically White Campuses: A Critical Race Examination of Race-related Stress." In *Faculty of Color Teaching in Predominantly White Colleges and Universities*, ed. C. A. Stanley (Bolton, MA: Anker, 2006): 299–327.

Smith, William, Walter Allen, and Lynette Danley, "'Assume the Position...You Fit the Description': Psychological Experiences and Racial Battle Fatigue Among African American Male College Students." *American Behavioral Scientist* 55, no. 44 (2007): 551–578.

Spelman, Elizabeth. *Inessential Woman: Problems of Exclusion in Feminist Thought* (Boston, MA: Beacon Press, 1988).

Spelman, Elizabeth. "Managing Ignorance." In *Race and Epistemologies of Ignorance*, eds. Shannon Sullivan and Nancy Tuana (Albany, NY: State University of New York Press, 2007): 119–131.

Srivastava, Sarita. "'You're Calling Me a Racist?' The Moral and Emotional Regulation of Antiracism and Feminism." *Signs: Journal of Women in Culture and Society* 31, no. 1 (2005): 29–62.

Staats, Cheryl. "Understanding Implicit Bias: What Educators Should Know." *American Educator* 39, no. 4, (2015–2016): 29–33.

Steele, Claude. *Whistling Vivaldi: How Stereotypes Affect Us and What We Can Do* (New York: W. W. Norton & Company, 2010).

Steele, Claude and Joshua Aronson. "Stereotype Threat and the Intellectual Test Performance of African-Americans." *Journal of Personality and Social Psychology* 69, no. 5 (1995): 797–811.

Sue, Derald Wing. *Microaggressions in Everyday Life: Race, Gender, and Sexual Orientation* (New York: Wiley and Sons, 2010).

Sue, Derald Wing, G. C. Torino, C. M. Capodilupo, D. P. Rivera, and A. I. Lin. "How White Faculty Perceive and React to Difficult Dialogues on Race: Implications for Education and Training." *The Counseling Psychologist* 37 (2009): 1090–1115.

Sullivan, Shannon. *Revealing Whiteness: The Unconscious Habits of Racial Privilege* (Bloomington, IN: Indiana University Press, 2006).

Tanesini, Alexandra. "Intellectual Humility as Attitude." *Philosophy and Phenomenological Research* 96, no. 2 (2018): 399–420.

Tao, Karen, Jesse Owen and Joanan Drinane. "Was *that* Racist? An Experimental Study of Microaggression Ambiguity and Emotional Reactions for Racial–Ethnic Minority and White Individuals." *Race and Social Problems* 9, no. 4 (2017): 262–271.

Tate, Shirley Ann and Damien Page, "Whiteliness and Institutional Racism: Hiding Behind (Un)conscious Bias." *Ethics and Education* 13, no. 1 (2018): 141–155.

Thomas, Owen. "Blind to Complicity? Official Truth and the Hidden Role of Methods." In *Exploring Complicity: Concept, Cases and Critique*, eds. Afxentis Afxentiou, Robin Dunford, and Michael Neu (New York and London: Rowman & Littlefield International, 2017): 161–178.

Thompson, Audrey. "Entertaining Doubts: Enjoyment and Ambiguity in White, Antiracist Classrooms." In *Passion and Pedagogy: Relation, Creation, and Transformation in Teaching*, eds. Elijah Mirochick and Debora C. Sherman (New York: Peter Lang, 2002): 431–452.

Thompson, Audrey. "Tiffany, Friend of People of Color: White Investments in Antiracism." *International Journal of Qualitative Studies in Education* 16, no. 1 (2003): 7–29.

Tschaepe. Mark. "Addressing Microaggressions and Epistemic Injustice: Flourishing from the Work of Audre Lorde." *Essays in the Philosophy of Humanism* 24, no. 1 (2016): 87–101.

TuSmith, Bonnie. "Out on a Limb: Race and the Evaluation of Frontline Teaching." In *Race in the College Classroom*, eds. Bonnie TuSmith and Maureen T. Reddy (New Brunswick, NJ: Rutgers University Press, 2002): 112–125.

Vice, Samantha. "How Do I Live in this Strange Place?" *Journal of Social Philosophy* 41, no. 3 (2010): 323–342.

Warren, Jonathan and France Winddance Twine, "White Americans, The New Minority? Non-Blacks and the Ever-Expanding Boundaries of Whiteness." *Journal of Black Studies* 28, no. 2 (1997): 20–218.

Wekheiser, Ian. "Asking for Reasons as a Weapon: Epistemic Justification and the Loss of Knowledge." *Journal of Cognition and Neuroethics* 2, no. 1 (2014): 173–190.

Wekker, Gloria. *White Innocence: Paradoxes of Colonialism and Race* (London: Duke University Press, 2017).

Whitcomb, Dennis, Heather Battaly, Jason Baehr, and Daniel Howard-Snyder, "Intellectual Humility: Owning our Limitations." *Philosophy and Phenomenological Research* 94, no. 3 (2017): 509–539.

Whitt, Matt. "Other People's Problems: Student Distancing, Epistemic Responsibility, and Injustice." *Studies in Philosophy of Education* 35 (2016): 427–444.

Yancy, George. *Backlash: What Happens When We Talk Honestly about Racism in America* (Lanham, MD: Rowman & Littlefield, 2018).

Yancy, George. *Black Bodies, White Gazes: The Continuing Significance of Race* (Lanham, MD: Lexington, 2008).

Yancy, George. "Dear White America." *The New York Times* (December 24, 2015).

Yancy, George and Todd May. "Policing is Doing What It was Meant to Do. That's the Problem." *New York Times*, June 21, 2020.

Index

active ignorance, 38–39, 45
affirmation, 111
Ahmed, Sarah, 11, 28–29, 46–48, 55, 89, 102, 123–24
Alcoff, Martin Linda, 125
all lives matter, 15
anti-racist education, 4, 30, 46, 49, 55, 58, 89, 96, 126
Asian-Americans, 100
attribution ambiguity, 100
Austin, J. L., 46

Baehr, Jason, 58, 74
Bailey, Alison, 11, 14–15, 70
Battaly, Heather, 58
bell hooks, 126
Berenstain, Nora, 68–72, 90, 92
Bialystok, Lauren, 74–75
black double consciousness, 125
Black Lives Matter, 15, 42, 70, 91, 102
"Black pat", 122
Blackwell, Deanna, 32, 96
boomerang discourse, 14
Bowman, Melanie, 68, 73
Bridges, Christopher, 56
Brookfield, Stephen, 55, 58, 91, 94, 98
Brown, Michael, 40
Brown v. Board of Education, 24

Callwood, June, 27
Case, Kim. *See* distancing strategies
Chinnery, Ann, 76, 80, 90, 92, 109
close-mindedness, 66
coerced self-silencing, 35
collective hermeneutical resources, 36
colorblind, 15, 39
color-evasiveness, 15
complicity, 7, 9, 109
consciousness raising, 49
critical feedback, 105, 108, 110
critical white double consciousness, 126
critical whiteness studies, 94
Croft, Alyssa, 103
cross-racial dialogues, 91–92
cross-racial feedback, 106
cultivating humility, 58
Curry-Stevens, Ann, 95

Daum, Courtenay, 49
Davidson, Kristie, 63
Davis, John W., 24
Davison, A., 110
Delgado, Didi, 126
Demetriou, Cynthia, 111
DiAngelo, Robin, 11, 64, 90, 95
Diaz, Jesus Jaime, 25
discursive strategies, 14

Index

distancing strategies, 13, 16, 45
diversity, 28–29
dominant hermeneutical frameworks, 36
Dotson, Kristie, 4, 34, 36, 62, 97, 100; epistemic oppression, 4
double bind, 32
double consciousness, 66, 126
Dozono, Tadashi, 76–77, 81, 110

echoing, 111
Ellis, James, 111
epistemic arrogance, 66
epistemic contributory, 38
epistemic exclusion, 62
epistemic exploitation, 41, 69–70, 72, 90, 97
epistemic friction, 39, 66–68
epistemic gaslighting, 40, 111
epistemic humility, 109
epistemic injustice, 17–18, 33, 36–37, 44, 56–57, 65, 76, 94, 96, 100, 107, 109–10
epistemic laziness, 66
epistemic oppression, 107
epistemic violence, 108
experiences of racism, 16

fantasy of transcendence, 64
Fatima, Saba, 39, 42, 100, 107
Fellows, Louise Mary, 27, 45, 97
feminist killjoy, 29, 123–24
Ferkany, Matt, 74–75
Floyd, George, 3–4
Frankenburg, Ruth, 69
Fricker, Miranda, 33, 35, 56, 60–61, 106
Frye, Marilyn, 64

gaslighting, 40, 42, 110
Gillborn, David, 3
Gilson, Erinn, 60
Glanville, Doug, 98–100
good intentions, 24
Gordon, Anna Jane, 126
Greco, John, 58

Hambrick, Angelica, 104
happy diversity talk, 28, 104
Hare, William, 73
Harris, Cheryl, 2
Harvin, Cassandra Byers, 35, 100
Hemmings, Annette. *See* distancing strategies
Henry, Paget, 126
hermeneutical injustice, 33, 35–36
Howard-Snyder, Daniel, 58
Huerta-Bapat, Carmen, 111
humility, 56; relational dimension, 60
Hytten, Kathy, 14, 99, 101

IBT. *See* implicit bias training
identity prejudice, 34, 56, 60–62, 82
identity privilege, 56
implicit bias, 56, 61–63, 82; implicit bias training, 57, 62–63
implicit identity bias, 24, 36–37
implicit knowledge, 102
inclusion, 28
individual deficiency, 38
individualist framework, 47
institutional racism, 102
institutional whiteness, 28
intellectual humility, 58
invulnerability, 78–79

Jones, Alison, 31–32, 91
Jun, Alexander, 104
justice oriented pedagogy, 78

kaleidoscope consciousness, 66
killjoy, 123
Kunstman, Jonathan, 103
Kwong, Jack, 74

Lamsma, Matthew, 104
Langston, Rae, 61
Leonardo, Zeus, 48, 91, 95, 102, 108, 115
Lodge-Eddo, Reni, 35
Logue, Jennifer, 78

Lorde, Audre, 30, 43, 71, 90, 101
"loving, knowing ignorance", 69

Major, Brenda, 103
Malta, Brenna, 103
marginalized epistemic framework, 42
marginalized students, 92
marginalized testimony, 41
Mason, Rebecca, 36
Mather, Peter, 56
Matias, Cheryl, 93
Maye, Carina, 91
Mayo, Cris, 68
McIntosh, Peggy, 95
McWhorter John, 11, 103, 113
Medina, Jose, 28, 39, 57, 60, 65–67, 112
Mendes, Berry Wendy, 103
meta-dialogue, 102
meta-ignorance, 39, 65
microaffirmations, 110–11
microaggressions, 98–102
microcompliments, 111
microinvalidation, 111
microsupports, 111
Mills, Charles, 3, 32, 38, 44, 65, 75; white supremacy, 3
Miranda, Francisco Dana, 126
multicultural imposter syndrome, 121
multicultural perfectionism, 121
multicultural projections, 121

ontological expansiveness, 10
open-mindedness, 73–74, 78
oppression, 64–65
Orozco, Richard, 25
Ortega, Marianna, 68–69
Ozlem, Sensoy, 90

Page, Damien, 63
Pander, A.T., 111
paradox of humility, 47
patterned absence, 101
pedagogy, 6, 17, 45, 58
performative utterances, 46

persistent deference, 38
personal narratives, 94
Phillips, Jennifer Akamine, 104, 122
Pohlhaus Jr, Gaile, 36–37, 40, 111–12
police brutality, 3
Porter, Ronald, 91, 108, 115
positive bias, 103
Power, Candice, 111
privilege, 4, 10, 39
Probyn, Fiona, 47

race, 2, 4, 26, 90, 106
race conscious, 33
racial battle fatigue, 12, 15, 41
racial injustice, 46, 56, 64, 99
racial microaggressions, 99
racial positionality, 25
racial stereotype threat theory, 106
racism, 25, 62, 98, 103
Razack, Sherene, 27, 45, 97
reasonableness, 42
reflexive questions, 6, 7
relationality of race, 90
relationality of whiteness, 1
resistance echoing, 112
rhetorical strategies, 14
Rich, Adrienne, 43, 71, 101
Richardson, Troy, 75
Riggs, Wayne, 74
Risdon, Nate, 104
Rolon-Dow, Rosalie, 110
Roman, Leslie, 32
Rombinson, Brian, 57
Ross, Thomas, 24
Rowe, Mary, 110

Sawyer, Pamela, 103
Schmander, Toni, 103
shadow text, 71, 83
silencing, 34
social identity, 62
social justice education, 32, 68, 76, 91, 96
social ontology, 9
Socrates, 57

Spellman, Elizabeth, 58
Srivastava, Sarita, 27–29
Steele, Claude, 105
stereotypes, 104, 106
stereotype threat, 105–7
structural identity privilege, 35
structural oppression, 16
structures of domination, 68, 73
structures of power, 9
Sue, Wing Derek, 99
Sullivan, Shannon, 10
survival echoing, 112
systemic racial injustice, 3, 10, 45, 48
systemic white ignorance, 24, 38
systemic white supremacy, 3, 11, 30, 44, 47, 90, 94, 121, 127

Tate, Shirley Anne, 63
Taylor, Rebecca, 76–77, 81, 110
testimonial injustice, 33
testimonial justice, 60–61
testimonial quieting, 34
testimonial sensibility, 60
testimonial smothering, 34
Thompson, Audrey, 4
Townsend, Sarah, 103

unconscious habits, 10
unearned white advantages, 48, 95
University diversity workers, 109
unknowing, 65
untethered relativism, 56

vulnerability, 60; susceptibility dimension, 79

Warren Jonathan, 2, 14, 99, 101
Wekheiser, Ian, 43, 71
Wekker, Gloria, 25–26

Whitcomb, Daniel, 58
white aspects of divergence, 8
white centered feminism, 27
white complicity, 2–3, 7–11, 16, 32, 44, 49, 103; denials of, 32
white connection, 8
white conventional approaches, 9
white discursive moves, 24
white double consciousness, 125–27
white educators, 4, 89, 93, 97, 101, 104, 107, 122; pedagogical challenges, 92–94
white exceptionalism, 27
white fragility, 64, 94–95
white innocence, 24–25, 27, 31, 44, 47, 90, 127
white inter-relationship, 9
whiteness, 2, 4, 10, 23, 69, 89–90, 98, 101, 125
whiteness of feminism, 16, 29
white privilege, 11, 40, 48–49, 95
white progressive resistance, 8
white racial consciousness, 126
whitesplaining, 42
white students, 89–90
white students complicity, 4
white supremacy, 3, 48
white talk, 14–16
white tears, 30
Whitt, Matt, 16, 38
willful ignorance, 24, 33, 36, 38–39, 41–45, 49, 56, 66, 73, 100, 108, 114, 122–23, 125, 127
Winddance Twine, France, 2
wokeness, 47
women of color: experiences, 30–31, 69

Yancy, George, 1, 3, 13, 23, 47, 55, 68–69, 75, 90, 99

About the Author

Barbara Applebaum is professor of Cultural Foundations of Education at Syracuse University. Although her training is in philosophy of education, her work and teaching are interdisciplinary in nature. Her academic research focuses on the ways in which whiteness is reproduced through education, especially in the guise of good intentions and, more specifically, within the context of social justice pedagogy. The journals in which her publications appear include *Hypatia, Philosophy of Education, Race, Ethnicity and Education*, and *Educational Theory*. Her recent work addresses such topics as the non-performativity of white virtue-signaling, challenging the comfort of white willful ignorance, a critique of implicit bias training on college campuses, and when comforting white discomfort is a form of complicity. Her book *Being White/Being Good: White Complicity, Responsibility and Social Justice Education* (2010) examines the meaning of white complicity, examines its ethical and epistemological assumptions, and offers recommendations for how white complicity can be named and disrupted.

www.ingramcontent.com/pod-product-compliance
Lightning Source LLC
Chambersburg PA
CBHW020126010526
44115CB00008B/986